The Training of Secondary School Heads In Western Europe

To Mary

The Training of Secondary School Heads In Western Europe

John Buckley
for
The Council of Europe

NFER-NELSON

Published by The NFER-NELSON PUBLISHING Company Ltd.,
Darville House, 2 Oxford Road East,
Windsor, Berkshire SL4 1DF

First published 1985
© The Council of Europe
ISBN 0 7005 06918
Code 8193 02 1

Set by Action Typesetting, Gloucester
Printed and bound in Great Britain
by Billing & Sons Limited, Worcester.

Distributed in the USA by Taylor & Francis Inc.,
242 Cherry Street, Philadelphia, PA 19106–1906.
Tel: (215) 238 0939. Telex: 244489

Contents

Acknowledgments   vii

Introduction   ix

Chapter 1: The Changing Role of the Secondary School
                 Head   1

Chapter 2: The Training Needs of Secondary Heads   27

Chapter 3: How Training Needs Are Being Met:
                 a series of case-studies   42
                 France   43
                 Sweden   60
                 England   80
                 The Netherlands   96
                 Norway   108

Chapter 4: Some Issues of Training Methodology   129

Chapter 5: Some Issues of Evaluation   153

Chapter 6: A Summary of Conclusions   168

Bibliography   185

Acknowledgments

During the preparation of this study very many individuals in different countries have made valuable contributions and to all of them I should like to express my very grateful thanks. I should like to thank in particular the following:

in England Lois Benyon, I. B. Butterworth, HMI., David Styan, Fred Tye, CBE, and R. A. Wake, HMI.

in France Monsieur C. Caré, Madame Marinette Peterson and Monsieur R. Wattiaux.

in Norway Brynhild Sirevåg and Oddvar Vormeland and

in Sweden Mats Ekholm, Nils Lagervall, Eskil Stegö and Bengt Thelin.

I also wish to express my gratitude and appreciation to my secretary, Barbara Card, for her valued help.

Over Peover,
Cheshire,
1984.

Introduction

There is now a rich European experience to be drawn upon in the field of training for management in secondary schools and it was with this in mind that the Council of Europe commissioned the above study, which took place during 1982 and 1983. The writer took part in a number of events during that period which were concerned with the training of heads and principals of secondary schools. These seminars and conferences were arranged by the international organizations the Council of Europe and the Commission of the European Communities, and also by teachers' professional associations: the Association for Teacher Education in Europe and the National Association of Head Teachers (in England). These meetings provided opportunities to encounter many individuals who are now holding appointments as heads or principals of schools in Europe or are engaged in the training of those who hold such posts.

The writer was head of a secondary school in England for thirteen years and then for eight years engaged in the training of heads and senior staff in schools. In addition to having been in close contact with many heads of schools in England he has also met during recent years groups of heads and of those responsible for training heads in France, the Federal Republic of Germany, Denmark, Iceland, Northern Ireland, Norway and Sweden, in the course of visits paid to these countries.

The approach of the study is a practical one and is based upon personal experience as a head and as a trainer of heads as well as upon the results of valuable encounters with others who are either heads of secondary schools themselves or are responsible for training heads of schools in their own countries. The study does not make any pretence of being an academic treatise and while reference is made to a number of research studies in the field, the conclusions are mainly personal and subjective.

Likewise, such a study cannot claim to be comprehensive because the field is so broad. Training in school management is one field of education which is expanding in Europe at a time when many other aspects of education systems are contracting. Inevitably, the study is selective and while it is hoped that significant developments in the member states at the time of writing have been identified, others are not mentioned, either through lack of space or because they have not been encountered by the writer.

However, it is hoped that sufficient experience and expertise have been gathered to offer some guidelines to those working in the field. These may be useful in a practical sense to those who may be contemplating setting up courses on the training of heads or who may wish to review their existing work in the field in the light of recent developments in other European countries. It is a particular hope that the study may be of some help to those countries which have little experience so far in training the senior staff of secondary schools and may wish to take advantage of the experience of others before embarking upon a programme of such training.

The first part of the study is an examination of some of the changes in the role of the head which are particularly significant during the present decade. Many of these changes are being brought about by the considerable pressures which are being exerted on schools from a variety of sources in society. A lasting impression derived from meetings with heads in a variety of European countries is of loneliness, of increasing day-to-day pressures and of a job that becomes more and more difficult. A series of quotations may serve to illustrate the state of mind of many heads of secondary schools:

'We struggle for survival in arctic conditions' (a head from England).
'How can a head be a politician and retain his integrity?' (a young deputy head from a village in Spain).
'In the present conditions the head is often the symbol of rejected values and a lonely person, abandoned by all and an object of aggression from all sides' (a headmistress from Belgium).
'Changes in society, including changes in attitudes of

pupils, of parents and of teachers towards the head and the constantly increasing demands of local and of central authorities, contribute to making the job more difficult' (an administrator from Denmark).

'You talk about objectives; my first objective on returning to school after a holiday is to replace most of the windows' (a head of a school in Northern Ireland).

'You talk about vision when I am submerged by paper' (a headmistress from France).

Such statements suggest vividly the situations in which many heads find themselves nowadays and the feelings which they experience in those situations. They serve as a timely reminder to those who are the providers of courses and of other forms of training that our first duty is to respond to the needs of those to whom the training is being offered. Training exists for the benefit of those being trained and not for the benefit of the trainers. An onus rests upon those responsible for training to begin where the heads 'are' and not where they would like them to be. This may mean going to considerable trouble to find out where they 'are', recognizing that the situation of each head and of each school is different and that it may well be appropriate to involve the heads themselves in the planning of their own training.

One point of departure of this study is, therefore, the position of the head as it is today. That position is seen as one in which the head is assailed on all sides by a wide variety of pressures and demands which often conflict one with another. These pressures may be both internal and external to the school. They may come from students, from parents, from teachers, from politicians, from trade unions, from employers, from the media or from other sources in the local community. The strength and force of those different pressures will vary from school to school, from locality to locality and from country to country, but there is a significant degree of consensus among the heads whom the writer has met about the states of mind induced by such pressures and the levels of stress which are generated by these frequently strident and often conflicting demands. The position of the contemporary head is one of considerable psychological insecurity. The provision of support and the building of confidence may be a priority to which the trainers should be giving a major emphasis.

However, while recognizing the immediate needs of heads which it is the responsibility of trainers both to understand and to attempt to meet in any programme of training, there are other needs which also have to be met and which may not appear so urgent as the acquisition of skills and strategies for coping with crisis but which are, in the view of the writer, equally important. These needs arise from the rapidly changing nature of the society in which we live. Social institutions are all being influenced by these changes and schools cannot expect to remain untouched. They too are changing and a significant role in this process of change is that played by the head. Consequently, a recognition of the head as an agent and indeed as a promoter of change is necessary by the heads themselves and by those responsible for their training. We are only just beginning to understand the complexity of the process of changing social institutions and in particular the process of changing schools. Nevertheless, some countries have already incorporated this element into their training programmes for heads. In Sweden, for example, the programme which has been developing since 1976 has always recognized the role of the head as a change agent. Eskil Stegö, one of those responsible for that programme, speaking at the Gatwick Conference in 1982 expressed this conviction:

> The basic assumption is that school leaders play an import-
> ant role in the development of a healthy school. He [the
> head] should in many ways be a change agent, or at least a
> facilitator of change. (ATEE and NAHT, 1982)

When an emphasis on that aspect of the head's role which is concerned with being a change agent is set beside the urgency and immediacy of solving everyday problems, or what is known as 'crisis management', then the major dilemma inherent in the job begins to emerge. On the one hand heads are engaged in a struggle for survival in the present, and on the other hand they have the responsibillity of developing the school for the future. In the first instance, they strive to achieve stability; in the second, they are expected to facilitate change which in its essence implies a degree of instability. Whereas in the past, while being head of a school was never a job characterized by tranquillity, at least periods of comparative stability tended to alternate with shorter periods of innovation. Now the pace of change has begun to accelerate, sometimes alarmingly. This situation gives rise to what the writer describes as the 'present-future' dilemma which faces many heads today and for which they are, in many instances, unprepared. Somehow they have to cope with a present which is volatile and full of problems and at the same time prepare for a future full of uncertainties which is rushing towards them. For example, it is genuinely difficult to predict how the technological revolution will have transformed schools or homes or factories in ten years' time. It is the management of this dilemma which the writer sees as a major task facing those who are responsible for schools during the next decade. A major need of heads is likely to be support, help and guidance in the resolution of the 'present-future' dilemma as it affects them in their own schools. This is not to imply that we must all become futurologists or indulge in the wilder excesses of science fiction. Speculation about the future is a hazardous operation and prophecy is even more dangerous. Nevertheless, those who are responsible for 'developing children and for developing schools need to devote much more attention to the future than they have done in the past.

An attempt is made to identify some of the training needs of those who have the responsibility of managing schools under these difficult conditions and a number of case studies are offered from different European countries which are attempting to meet these needs. Some consideration is given to the issues of appropriate training methodology and of evaluation. A summary of conclusions is provided.

In the course of this study the writer attended the following events concerned with the training of heads and principals of secondary schools:

The international conference on 'Training for heads (school leaders) in Europe' which took place at Gatwick in the United Kingdom from March 12th to 14th 1982. This conference was arranged by the National Association of

Head Teachers in collaboration with the Association for Teacher Education in Europe.

The Council of Europe Teachers' Seminar on 'Current trends in school management', which was held in Kristiansand, Norway, from August 9th to 14th 1982.

The Council of Europe Research Workshop on 'Training for management in schools' which was arranged in collaboration with the National Foundation for Educational Research and took place at Windsor in the United Kingdom from September 14th to 17th 1982.

The conference arranged by the French Ministry of Education for the Commission of the European Communities on 'School for the 11–14 age range and its priority tasks' which took place at Pont-à-Mousson in France from November 7th to 13th 1982. One of the four sub-themes of this conference was 'The in-service training of school leaders'.

CHAPTER 1

The Changing Role of the Secondary School Head

Some views of heads themselves

If one talks to heads from different countries about their jobs, it becomes apparent that they do not have a simple definition of their role. When asked what they do, heads tend to emphasize the fragmented and discontinuous nature of the job. They say that they seldom have time to provide carefully thought-out responses to questions that are put to them or to work out carefully planned solutions to problems that face them. They talk of the lack of time to do the job properly, either because of the amount of administrative paper work in some countries or because of the number of bureaucratic procedures in other countries. Those who follow the routine of compiling a list of outstanding things to be done by the end of the day speak of the common experience of reaching the end of the day with more items on the list than there were at the beginning, and consequently taking some of their work home with them. There seems to be too little time for reflection, thinking and planning. Wherever they come from there is reference to the number of different face-to-face meetings every day, the number of verbal encounters engaged in. These may often be with a wide diversity of people from both inside and outside their schools: professional and non-professional; teachers, students, parents, employers, advisers, inspectors, old, young and middle-aged.

Many heads describe the complexity and the confusion which exists about their role, the changes which that role has undergone in the past decade and indeed which it continues to undergo in the present, whether brought about by increased decentralization as in Norway, Sweden or in France or by falling rolls as in Great Britain, or by demands for more democracy as in Spain and in Italy. The discussion groups at the Gatwick Conference in 1982 found a remarkable degree of common ground in the complexity of the head's task: 'There are differences in role between the various countries, but in all cases the range of duties is complex and subject to constant changes' (ATEE and NAHT, 1982).

In the more centralized systems such as France, Italy, Belgium, Luxembourg, Greece, Germany and Denmark, ministry directives affect such matters as curriculum and organization. Pautler, in her paper to the EEC seminar (1982) reported a common emphasis on the weight of bureaucracy and the amount of paper work. There are many circulars to be read, understood and interpreted at the local level. An increased knowledge of the law is now required in Denmark and in the Federal Republic of Germany. She also stresses the increased influence of parents who sit on school committees in France, Sweden and Denmark, on what are known as governing bodies in England and Wales, and who have recourse to tribunals in the case of grievances in Germany.

A head (Skoglund, 1982) reporting on the effects of decentralization in Sweden to the Teachers' Seminar at Kristiansand emphasized how the trade unions have increased their pressures on heads:

> Trade unions have assumed a stronger position which means that the employer is bound to inform employees of all questions and negotiate about certain questions. These circumstances have strikingly increased the amount of work to be done by the head. In cases which I have formerly settled in my solitude and by virtue of my wisdom, I have now to call a meeting. Sometimes, I have to call several meetings. (Council of Europe, 1982).

A number of heads have been seconded from their jobs in England to study the role of the head. Jackson (1976) identified among the salient features 'the unrelenting call for adaptation to constant change, excessive paperwork and above all the high personal stress of the head's job'. Schofield (1980) when seconded to the institution where the writer worked, to study the factors contributing to the creation of a successful comprehensive school, found that heads had to deal with a wide variety of unplanned tasks, cope with many interruptions and external pressures and face crisis problems requiring an immediate response (p.48). Nockels was seconded to examine the problems of the first year of secondary headship. A new head taking up an appointment nowadays is particularly vulnerable to those pressures coming from outside the school for which an academic training has not provided any appropriate preparation:

> Whether teachers in general and heads in particular like it or not, more people are going to take an informed interest in what is going on in schools and more will be prepared to express an opinion whenever and wherever they think fit than has ever been the case before. Upon occasions, too, this opinion will be forced upon the schools and sometimes upon the whole educational structure of an area in opposition to the view held by the head and his staff . . . This readiness to express an opinion which can be given wide publicity by press and television is something new to our age (Nockels, 1981).

These last three examples are from studies carried out by practising heads in England where the tradition has been for heads to enjoy considerable autonomy and independence compared with many of their colleagues in other European countries, whose education systems are more centralized. The writer's own encounters with heads in a variety of European countries reinforce these conclusions that the role of the head is becoming more complex and difficult to define and that this increase in complexity may often be attributed to diverse outside influences which are affecting schools. Some heads express their need to acquire skills in public relations, others refer to the need for what Glatter has described as 'marketing skills'. Others again are more conscious of the political pressures and the need to develop an appropriate stance and an appropriate vocabulary to understand and deal with such outside influences. Furthermore, they claim that these outside influences make increased demands on their time, creating pressures and increasing personal stress. One consequence of this trend is that some heads are unable to devote the time they would wish to what they refer to as the 'educational aspects' of their job or to the pedagogical leadership of their schools. Such a trend is particularly significant at a time when a number of countries visited by the writer such as Denmark, France and Sweden are carrying out or planning to carry out changes in their curriculum which will be far-reaching and long-term in their effects. Indeed, the need for heads to be concerned and involved in educational innovation and yet having to give more attention to 'management' is given by some as a factor which renders the job more difficult. A head from the Netherlands reported,

> It may be safely said that the job has become increasingly more difficult. Among possible causes are:
> — educational innovations
> — a shift of emphasis from pedagogical–didactic matters to problems concerning management.

These views of heads suggest a diversifying of the heads' concerns, an increased work-load and consequently less time to devote to what may be described as 'educational matters'. Some psychological effects of these developments in the heads' role are to increase pressure, create a sense of insecurity and induce loneliness. Pautler (1982) describes the situation of the recently-appointed heads in those countries where their responsibilities are not shared with a team of deputy heads and senior teachers thus:

> The solitude and inexperience of new heads who are former teachers, who for the most part have no special aptitudes for the tasks of headship and who are frequently unaware of the multiple roles implied by their new job, often give rise to anxiety.

Schofield (1980) finds clear evidence that these changes have influenced heads' leadership styles and the managerial structures of schools:

4

> The increased complexity of schools has made it necessary
> for heads to abandon their attempts to run the schools
> single-handed ... In many schools heads have voluntarily
> relinquished some of their traditional powers in favour of a
> more participatory style of management (p. 13).

Such modifications in the heads' role have been relatively
more possible in England where in a large comprehensive
secondary school there may be as many as three deputy heads
and other senior teachers. In those countries where the
management structures do not include a number of such senior
appointments, it is understandable that feelings of isolation,
insecurity, anxiety and stress are likely to be much greater.

The evidence of this first part of the study of the changing
role of the head in a European context has been drawn, for the
most part, from direct contact with practising heads or from
contact with those responsible for their training. It presents a
somewhat confused picture in which the role appears to be
difficult to describe clearly and certainly not simply. More
often heads describe their states of mind, their own confusions
and anxieties, and a multiplicity of tasks. It may be
appropriate to conclude this part of the study by a summary of
some of those changes in the role of the head which were
identified by the groups working at Kristiansand (1982) which
represented fifteen European countries. These changes were
identified in all the countries represented with particular
emphasis in certain countries as indicated.

1. A greater need for consultation with teachers, parents
   and pupils, particularly in Sweden, Norway, the Federal
   Republic of Germany, Belgium, Portugal and in the UK
2. More accountability to the local community, particularly
   in Sweden, Portugal and the UK
3. Problems arising from economic recession and from
   increasing unemployment, particularly in the Federal
   Republic of Germany, France and the UK
4. A general increase in work load and a diversification of
   tasks, particularly in Sweden and in the UK
5. A move towards more decentralization particularly in
   France, Sweden and Norway

    6. A need to become more effective in human relations both within the school and externally.

This summary of changes taking place in the role of of the head represents a remarkable degree of consensus that the majority of such changes are being brought about by influences outside the schools. Heads in all the member states feel pressures, in some cases very urgent and in many cases expressed in formal directives to become more responsive to the demands of society and to become more open to the expectations of society. There are, on the one hand, demands by society to set alternative aims for schools and, at the other end of the educative process, demands by society to evaluate the product in order to ascertain whether the aims have been met. It is not the purpose of this study to explore in depth the relationship between schools and society. Such a vast subject is beyond the scope of this study. Nevertheless, the importance of certain changes in this relationship cannot be ignored when considering the role of the head and the training of those who play that role. If schools are being asked to perform a different task by society than has traditionally been the case then the role which the head is asked to play may also be very different. It may suffice to quote in this context the words of Pierre Vanbergen in his paper 'The School and its Relations with the Community' when he addressed the European Conference of Ministers of Education (Strasbourg 1977):

> For various reasons, which are simultaneously social, philosophical and intellectual, the care of our education systems developed historically in Europe in association with what is commonly called classical humanism, as a form of teaching detached from the contingent world outside and devoted to the pursuit of all that is stable and permanent in man and nature. On this model, the school has been considered in the West as an institution whose ability to function depended on how well it could keep its distance from the world. To safeguard its serenity, it readily effected detachment with regard to the problems of the day and organized itself in a closed environment, protected from the realities, by developing a 'neutral culture'. Thus, it came to

regard itself as an institution with its own objectives, not necessarily in keeping with the community's expectations and requirements.

Many heads and many teachers in different European countries are devoting much time and skill to the task of breaking down the barriers which exist between schools and society but the process is long and painful. The voices calling for change are discordant and the demands often conflict. It is genuinely difficult for those who are faced with the day-to-day problems of schools to build a coherent picture of the expectations and demands even of a local community, let alone an understanding of the much wider social developments such as the growing demands for a genuine share in decision-making, the extraordinary advances in information technology or the evolution of a multi-cultural society. This genuine difficulty in coping with the demands of the immediate present while at the same time engaging in reflection and in predictive thinking about the future is a persistent theme of this study. It is described by the writer as the 'present-future' dilemma.

The views of some researchers

This study began by considering, for the most part, the views of heads themselves, either those encountered by the writer himself or views gathered by others who have either met and talked to heads or assembled information by administering questionnaires seeking heads' views on their roles or on their training needs. The study has hopefully begun where heads 'are'.

However, this is only one point of departure. The role may be looked at by others and during the courses and seminars attended by the writer in 1982, other significant views were expressed by those with a research background in the training of heads. This was particularly so at the Windsor workshop, which whilst it was primarily concerned with research in the field of training for management in schools, in fact devoted considerable time to the changing role of the head, if only because it established fairly quickly that, apart from work carried out in Sweden (which will be referred to later in this study) there is very little existing research in the field of training for management in schools.

If we consider first the 'often frantic succession of disconnected and varied activities' which characterizes a head's work and to which the heads themselves often refer, this is not, in fact, peculiar to heads but was typical of the chief executives studied by Mintzberg as long ago as 1973 in his seminal work carried out by structured observational techniques. Mintzberg dispelled the myth that senior managers spent their time planning, organizing, co-ordinating and controlling. Far from being reflective, systematic planners:

> Managers work at unrelenting pace. Their activities are characterised by brevity, variety and discontinuity. They are strongly oriented to action and dislike reflective activities. (p.50)

Hughes in his paper to the Windsor workshop (in Hegarty, (Ed) 1983) described two observational studies of the work of high school principals, one in the United States (Martin and Willower, 1981) and the other in Australia (Willis 1980), both applying the techniques used by Mintzberg. The American study was of five principals who were under continuous observation in their schools for one week and the Australian study similarly involved structured observation of school principals in three schools over three weeks. The American study demonstrates several characteristics: the volume and pace of the work load; its variety, brevity and fragmentation; the preference of the principals for live action, priority going to tasks that require immediate attention, and could be dealt with quickly. Much of the above is confirmed in detail by the Australian study and Hughes notes the similarity of both to studies carried out in England, notably the extensive study carried out by Lyons (1972, 1976). An analysis was made of records kept by heads, senior teachers, bursars and secretaries for one week in each of three terms. Specially devised diaries were used as were small tape recorders as memory aids. Sixteen schools were involved and the daily pattern again emerged as one of a hectic, fragmented series of activities. Lyons (1972) comments:

It is difficult to find a quantifiable index which reflects with any degree of accuracy the pace and pressures of work at certain parts of the school day or term. Events impinge one upon another and interruptions are in turn interrupted. (p.27)

Heads on average dealt with some 40 unanticipated events in one week. Although many events are of short duration it cannot be assumed that they are unimportant. Work needing long uninterrupted periods of time was of necessity left to evenings or to weekends. The time spent out of school hours by heads on administrative activities was 14·5 hours per week on average.

Hughes (op.cit.) concludes that

Given the distinct historical, governmental and social context of education in England and Wales, in the United States and in Australia, it may be expected that there are significant differences in corresponding role conceptions for the school head or principal. Whatever differences there may be, however, it appears that there is considerable similarity in the work activity and managerial behaviour across the continents, and that in important respects task performance is very similar to that of chief executives in other types of work organizations. (p.35).

Michael Fullan (1982) is a valuable source on the way principals in the United States and Canada spend their time according to the researchers. His work is particularly relevant to this study because it is concerned with educational change and how it is implemented. He examines the role of the principal in the process of educational change and begins this part of his study (Chapter 8) by asserting that 'the role of the principal has in fact become more complex, overloaded and unclear over the past twenty years' (p. 130). The principal's day is taken up with one-to-one personal encounters, meetings, and telephone calls. Weldy (1979) describes how high school principals spend their days. He presents a time log for a typical day of one principal which shows a continuous stream of one-to-one interactions, telephone calls and administrative details which occur in one minute to fifteen minute 'clips' all day long.

Fullan makes the following significant point about the pressures under which principals now work.

> If change is everywhere in the air, we would think that the greatest pressure a principal feels is to bring about some major transformation of the school. But the air is not the ground, and on the ground many principals experience (and some people may say too easily accept) precisely the opposite — pressures to *maintain stability.* (p.131).

Sarason (1971) shows that most of the principals' time is spent on administrative housekeeping matters and maintaining order. Many principals expect to or feel that they are expected to keep everyone happy by running an orderly school, and this becomes a major criterion of the principal's ability to manage — no news is good news, as long as everything is relatively quiet.

House and Lapan (1978) express the preoccupation of the principal thus:

> The principal has no set of priorities except to keep small problems from becoming big ones. His is a continuous task of crisis management. He responds to emergencies daily. He is always on call. All problems are seen as important. This global response to any and all concerns means he never has the time, energy or inclination to develop or carry out a set of premeditated plans of his own. Containment of all problems is his theme. The principal cannot be a change agent or leader under these conditions. (p.145).

Fullan instances another large scale survey of principals in the United States carried out by Byrne *et al.*, (1978). This sample of 1131 principals was asked to rate how essential certain types of pre- or in-service courses were to their work. The authors compared the results with those of a similar survey carried out twelve years earlier and reported the following:

Course	1977 Rated essential	1965 Rated essential
School law	77%	32%
Curriculum development	76%	41%
School management	74%	26%
Human relations	71%	45%
Administrative theory and practice	32%	41%

The overall amount and range of essential knowledge as seen by principals has increased in five of the six categories. This increased knowledge requirement may reflect what principals see as problems of increased work-load and the need for role clarification. Issues of curriculum development which may be seen as one form of change and also issues which concern maintenance of stability show quite dramatic increases. Fullan writes,

> Even more interesting in the same survey is the rank ordering of how principals 'do spend their time' compared to how they think they 'should spend time'. Curriculum development was ranked 5 out of nine tasks in terms of 'do' and 1 out of nine in terms of 'should'. (p.133).

Similar findings are reported by Fullan himself on time spent in a representative sample of Ontario principals (Eastabrook and Fullan 1978). 44 per cent of the principals said that they actually spend a great deal of time on curricular tasks, while 76 per cent indicated that they would ideally like to spend a great deal more time on such tasks. The percentages were reversed for administrative tasks (paperwork, meetings etc.). Similarly, Hill *et al.* (1980) in a study of how federal programmes affect the principal's role found that paperwork took up 25 per cent of the principal's work week (ranging from 10 per cent to 50 per cent among the 55 principals in the sample). Principals reported that their roles had become more demanding; busier, less autonomous and more complex than they had been five years ago: administrative work, consultation with parents, involvement with students over discipline had all increased significantly. Nothing had decreased except that they spent slightly less time on supervising the teaching process. They spent less on teaching issues than they wanted to.

Fullan sums up his assessment of the principal's present position by stating:

> There should be no doubt that unless special steps are taken (by the principal and others), the principal has no time to be an educational leader. More and more responsibilities have been added to the role without any being taken away. (p.134)

The evidence offered by Fullan from an American and Canadian background reinforces the 'present-future' dilemma faced by heads and principals on both sides of the Atlantic. The role is becoming overloaded, the complexity and multiplicity of the tasks is increasing and there is considerable pressure from within the school, quite justifiable pressure, to maintain a stable ethos. There is insufficient time to devote to reflection and planning for the future, in particular to undertaking curriculum development. There exists some conflict and tension between the role of the head as administrator and the head as innovator or change agent.

Hughes in his paper to the Windsor workshop (in Hegarty (Ed), 1983) gave an account of his own work in this field in England (1972, 1973, 1975 and 1977). This work sought to test out the proposition that the secondary school head . is simultaneously 'the leading professional' and 'the chief executive' of his organization; that is, he is an example of an interesting phenomenon, the professional-as-administrator. Some of the major findings were as follows.

1. The empirical evidence relating to the leading professional aspect of the role revealed two independent factors: firstly, a *traditional* factor which could be indentified with the older 'headmaster tradition'; secondly, an *innovating* factor, indicating an openness to external professional influences leading to educational change.

2. The independence of the two factors suggests a four-fold typology: an individual head may be
   (a) below average on both dimensions: an *abdicator;*
   (b) below average on one dimension but not the other: a *traditionalist* or an *innovator;*
   (c) above average on both dimesions: an *extended professional.* (p.25).

These findings provide a very useful framework and conceptual basis for considering the present role of the head. In the English tradition, the role is seen to have evolved from the 'benevolent autocrat', who had his origins in the English public schools of the mid-nineteenth century, through the development of a more managerial and bureaucratic approach in the 1970's, to the notion of the dual nature of the role in the 1980s. Both aspects of the role are now recognized as significant, the traditional concerned with stability, smooth running and accountability and the innovative concerned with the development of the school in the context of continuous social and environmental change.

What this writer seeks to explore when considering the provision of appropriate training programmes in a European context is the tension and indeed conflict which may exist between these two equally important aspects of the role of the head. In the dynamic situation of school life a head does not calmly and reflectively decide to assume the role of the 'extended professional'. He may find himself torn between competing demands for stability and for innovation. He is often in the position described by Fullan (op.cit.), being

> ... buffeted as the teacher is by wanted and unwanted and often incomprehensible changes — and what is more, expected to lead these very changes. Change is only one small part of the forces competing for the principal's attention, and usually not the most compelling one ... The principal is in the middle of the relation between teachers, external ideas and people. As in most human triangles there are constant conflicts and dilemmas. (p.130)

Again, it is the external nature of the influences and

pressures which is emphasized here: the extended professional must now extend his professionalism outside his own professional circle. He or she will often have to deal nowadays with a confused cacophony of demands for change (or for stability) not always expressed in professional terms.

This recognition of the extent to which external factors are increasingly influencing the role of the head has emerged also in the work of Morgan and Hall (1982). They undertook a three-year research project at the Open University in England on the procedures in appointing heads in the UK and have studied the role of the head in the process. When embarking upon their project they began by analysing the common or generic elements in all secondary headships. They first set out a description of what they called the *managerial policy tasks* and the *managerial role relationships.* These two analyses are set out in Tables 1 or 2 and the researchers claim that they have received good support from serving heads, advisers and LEA officers in England. Secondly, they suggest an approach to defining what is *specific* rather than *generic* to any particular headship.

As a means of classifying all the tasks for which heads carry responsibility they used Katz's (1974) classical analysis of chief executive managerial roles which has three major task categories:

1. Technical tasks concerned with the special activity of the organization, e.g. educating children.
2. Conceptual tasks concerned with the overall running and controlling of the organization, e.g. planning, organizing, co-ordinating and controlling.
3. Human relations tasks concerned with all aspects of the management of people.

However, they thought it necessary to add an additional fourth category for some tasks of headship which could have been accommodated in one of the 'Katz categories' but which seemed to constitute, in the case of schools, a distinct group, namely:

4. External management tasks.

Task Category	Sub Task		Definition
Technical, i.e. Educational	1	Goal idenficiation	Identifying and deciding in concert with all interested parties, overall school aims and objectives.
	2	Academic Curriculum	Deciding a curriculum relevant to the academic abilities and needs of all pupils, and allocating curricular responsibilities to departments, staff members and pupils.
	3	Pastoral Curriculum	Deciding a policy and organization for pupils' pastoral care.
	4	Ethos	Deciding the school ritual and norms of behaviour and discipline for pupils and staff.
	5	Resources	Selection and appointment of staff, allocation of capitation allowances, determination of posts above Scale 1, and control of school funds and budget generally.
Conceptual, i.e. Operations Management	6	Planning, organization, co-ordination and control	Determination of the rules, responsibilities and mechanisms for all internal school policy making and management control, including the delegated responsibilities of the senior management team. Externally co-ordinating the school's provision with feeder schools and the needs of FE and HE colleges.
	7	Staff deployment	Defining staff tasks and writing job descriptions.
	8	Evaluation and record keeping	Evaluating effective standards of teaching in the classroom and progress on all aspects of school policy generally by establishing criteria and instruments for assessment and judgment. Compiling returns, monitoring the keeping of registers and statistical records.
	9	Buildings, ground and plant	Supervision, security and maintenance of the physical plant.
Human Relations i.e. Leadership and Human Management	10	Motivation	Motivating staff and pupils by personal influence, incentives, and concern for individual needs, health, safety and working conditions generally.
	11	Staff development	Developing policy and mechanisms for the professional development, work enrichment and technical support of staff.
	12	Inter-personal, intra-group and inter-group conflict resolution	Solving problems and resolving conflict by applying chairmanship, negotiation, arbitration, and reconciliation skills.
	13	Communication	Securing the effective dissemination of school policy, news of activities and events, and effective channels of two-way communication.
External Management, i.e. Community Relations and Accountability	14	Accountability to governors and LEA	Attending and reporting to Governors' meetings, liaising with the chairman, and embracing governors' views on school policy and achieving their consent and support. Working in accordance with LEA policy and establishing mechanisms for curricular and other technical advice from LEA officers and advisers.
	15	Parents and the general community	Determining a policy to achieve the support and involvement of parents in the running of the school. Presenting news of the school to the local community and gauging community expectations of the school.
	16	Employers and external agencies	Establishing communication with employers concerning their expectations and employment opportunities, and linking the school with supporting external agencies.

Table 1: Managerial tasks of the secondary school head

© Longman. This table is reproduced from *Education*, 18 June 1982, with kind permission of the editor and Colin Morgan and Valerie Hall of the Open University.

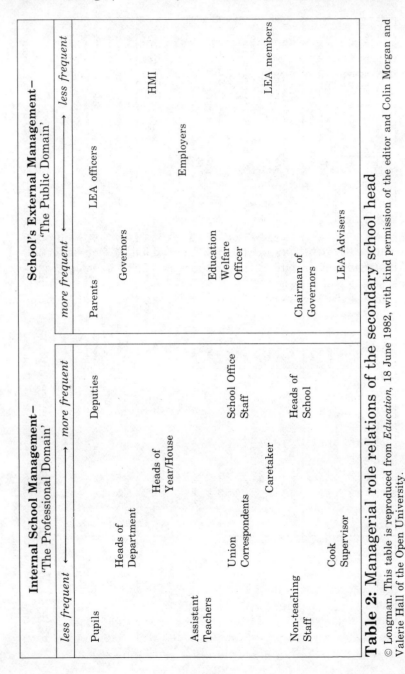

Table 2: Managerial role relations of the secondary school head

© Longman. This table is reproduced from *Education*, 18 June 1982, with kind permission of the editor and Colin Morgan and Valerie Hall of the Open University.

They considered schools as part of a wider system of educational government and as having more substantial and complex inter-relationships with the wider community than is the case with other types of organizations. Consequently, the demands for accountability are pervasive and various and impose a specific set of external management tasks on the head of a school.

There are a number of implications which arise from this analysis of the head's managerial tasks.

The first category (sub-tasks 1–5) calls for specifically professional knowledge and expertise relating to schools, pupils, teachers and education, while categories two and three (sub-tasks 6–13) call for knowledge and skills which Katz sees as generic to senior management everywhere. The fourth category which Morgan and Hall have added, namely external management, again introduces factors which are specific to schools. The analysis is useful in distinguishing the generic and specific aspects of the heads' role and supports the notion of the head as both 'leading professional' and 'chief executive' of the school.

In Table 2 Morgan and Hall offer a further useful analysis of the head's relationships with individuals and groups, i.e. the head's role set. This is divided into two distinct parts: the Professional Domain and the Public Domain. There are the groups internal to the school with whom the head has been familiar throughout his professional career. On the other hand there are groups of people external to the school with whom a head must work and with whom he will not be familiar. These people will include some educationists such as inspectors, advisers and education officers but this external or public domain includes many more 'non-educational' groups such as parents, employers, politicians and others who may only possess a lay knowledge of pupils, teachers and education. In this public domain the head has a responsibility for communication, interpretation, explanation, negotiation and accountability which when compared with the responsibilities of his previous career is likely to be a new experience. Some heads reported to the researchers that they perceived the demands from the public domain to have grown substantially in recent years. They also pointed out that in addition to these

17

increasing external demands for accountability there were parallel increasing internal pressures for more open management within the school and the emergence of pressure groups with an interest in promoting particular curriculum matters. They also stressed the increasing role played by trade unions.

Morgan and Hall see two important implications arising from these developments in the head's role set. The first is that the expectations from these different groups may differ dramatically and could well contradict. Role conflict and ambiguity are now an element in the job of being a head and there is a political task of balancing and mediating different expectations and demands, interpreting one group to another and achieving consensus. Secondly, the researchers see this divide in the head's role set between the professional and public domains as an 'hour glass' with the head at the neck receiving pressure from the familiar internal influences and from external influences much less familiar to him in terms of any specialized programme of training. They see the skills required in these circumstances as largely exclusive to headship and only fortuitously developed in the career path. These skills include brokerage and judgment, an ability to resolve conflict and ambiguity and also the capacity to communicate effectively with non-professionals, whose views of reality and whose vocabularies may be very different from those of the groups residing within the heads' professional domain.

Having thus distinguished between generic tasks and role relations, Morgan and Hall proceed to seek conceptual clarity on the issue of what individual properties of a school might need to be added to a generic job description. They use the construct of 'the situation' as a means of isolating the contextual factors of history, social background and special needs which make an individual school unique. They suggest two clear 'situation' dimensions on which a school's specific characteristics can be assembled:

1. Socio-cultural factors: e.g. whether the school is an inner-urban or rural school, whether the school is a multi-ethnic institution or whether the school serves an area

ethnic institution or whether the school serves an area with specific problems such as unemployment or crime.

2. School policy factors and management needs: e.g. whether there are key features of curriculum, organization, ethos or staff morale which need to be taken into consideration when making the appointment of a head to a particular school.

The researchers suggest that while the 'situation' and individual characteristics are important, great weight is often given by selectors to 'specifics', to the total exclusion of the 'generics'. They stress that the 'situation' of a school may be much more dynamic than constant and suggest that heads should be selected for their versatility, keeping the generic job skills central in both training and selection for headship.

While the work of Morgan and Hall and the POST project, as it is known in England, has been concerned with the selection procedures used for appointing heads of secondary schools, the view of secondary headship which they present is a valuable contribution to the understanding of that role. They indicate a number of skills which heads need to develop: professional, managerial, social and political; they emphasize the increasing importance of external influences and pressures and the parallel growth of internal pressures and they also stress the 'situation' factors which make each school different and therefore the role of every head different.

A further useful framework for considering both the role of the head as well as the process of training was put forward by Glatter in his paper to the Windsor workshop (in Hegarty (Ed), 1983). He devoted considerable attention to the notion of 'effectiveness' in school management. In presenting his thoughts on effectiveness in relation to the planned development of heads, Glatter proposes the helpful framework of three elements which might inform such development. These elements are:

1. An analysis of skills needed for the job.
2. An analysis of the pressures and dilemmas to which the job is subject.
3. An awareness of the ways in which the job is changing in response to contemporary developments.

In relation to the first of these elements, the question of skills, he refers to the ambitious attempt to define these for diagnostic purposes in a USA context by the National Association of Secondary School Principals (NASSP). He emphasizes the apparent agreement among a number of researchers and practitioners concerning the great importance of human skills, particularly communication and listening skills and the ability to relate to a wide range of different kinds of people, quoting from Gorton and McIntyre (1978):

> Effective principals seem to understand people, know how to motivate them, and how to deal effectively with their problems. It is primarily this factor, rather than technical expertise, that causes 'the significant others' to perceive these principals as accessible and effective administrators.

However, Glatter points to the limitation of such task analyses because they may tend to operate 'in a vacuum' and with little reference to relationships. Hence his second element in understanding the job, namely, the study of the pressures to which it is subject (also stressed by Morgan and Hall) and in particular the conflicting interests and expectations of the different participants such as parents or trade unions. Glatter has written elsewhere of the 'micropolitics' of the school and the implications for planned development of recognizing the political forces within an educational institution (see Hegarty, 1983). He has also written of the everyday pressures on senior staff in a variety of educational contexts in the UK, such as the fragmented work pattern, the continual interruptions and the need to 'change gear' quickly and frequently (Glatter 1972 and 1981). This can have an impact on job satisfaction, health and overall effectiveness unless heads are equipped by personality and/or by development to cope with it. However, it is Glatter's third area of interest which is particularly significant to this study. He introduces a further dimension to our understanding of the head's role which concerns contemporary developments, the changing nature of the role and the capacity of the head to deal with the future. Staff expect their leaders to give a sense of purpose, direction and coherence to their schools. Teachers find disorganization and inefficiency extremely frustrating.

The significance of this 'sense of direction' is also pointed out by Rutter *et al.* (1979). Yet Glatter points out that studies suggest that the activity pattern of managers breeds in them a disinclination to give attention to longer term planning, witness the description by Martin and Willower (1981):

> All the principals demonstrated a tendency to engage themselves in the most current and pressing situations. They invested little time in reflective planning ... Priority usually went to tasks that required immediate action or could be quickly completed.

This concern about the importance of long-term planning and of future development leads Glatter to conclude that while the analysis of tasks is important there is another important element in the role, namely resourcefulness and creativity:

> It should not become so dominant that a mechanistic approach to planned development emerges. The contemporary school leader and his/her senior colleagues need to be highly resourceful in coping with an increasingly turbulent environment (Bush and Gethins, 1981) in a complex reality, they need to generate initiatives and solutions which are usually not found within a standard set of techniques. Techniques have had only limited application within educational management and planned development must always find ways of stimulating rather than inhibiting resourcefulness in school managers. (p.111).

Creativity and imagination in the make-up of managers is the possession of what is described in a study of one private company as a 'helicopter quality',

> the ability to detach oneself from the immediate task, to look at problems from a higher vantage point and to see their interconnections with adjoining activities — to see the wood and the trees simultaneously. This is closely related with imagination, power of analysis, and a sense of reality. (Foy, 1979),

It is this capacity for creativity and imagination, and this writer would add the word *vision,* in relation to change and to the future, combined with a realistic awareness of the present with all its pressures and constraints which appears to be a potent element in resolving the 'present-future' dilemma and therefore deserving of major attention in any study of training for headship.

In his address to the European Teachers' Seminar 'Current trends in school management' at Kristiansand (1982), the writer introduced the 'present-future' dilemma by making three assumptions:

(a) that most schools are being managed for today, a number for yesterday;
(b) that some schools are being managed for tomorrow, and
(c) that very few schools are being managed for the day after tomorrow. (p.5).

The paper then developed this theme in three parts. Firstly, school management needs to take much more account of the future than is now the case. It is not possible for heads to ignore the 'premature arrival of the future'. Secondly, schools will still need to be managed for the immediate present. Crisis management will continue to be a norm. The maintenance of stability will still be necessary. Thirdly, and perhaps the most difficult task, is that of negotiating from where we are now, to where we want to be in the future. The management of the change is thus constrained by the complexities of the present. This negotiation of transition from a very difficult present to a very uncertain future represents a significant shift of emphasis in the role of the head. The major problem facing heads both now and for the foreseeable future is not managing the present or planning for the future. It is not a matter of choice. The problem is managing the present while preparing for the future at the same time. The study of the 'long-term future' as it affects or will affect a particular school becomes a managerial task requiring the creativity and imagination referred to by Glatter. This study of the 'day after tomorrow' may well help to solve some of the problems of tomorrow, and may even reduce some of the confusion of today. Hopefully, it will shed some light on which innovations should be embarked upon and which should be ignored. Changes which are affecting society are inevitably going to affect schools and heads will play a most significant role as change-agents in managing those changes. Some of these changes will originate from outside the school and the head will find that he or she is under pressure to implement them. There may well be conflicting pressures to implement contradictory changes and it is for this reason that the study of the 'long-term future' is offered as an additional dimension to the contemporary and future role of the head. The future will need to be planned for strategically and 'mapped' systematically, and to be enabled to undertake such planning heads will require training.

In identifying the qualities possessed by successful heads in their study of 'Ten Good Schools' Her Majesty's Inspectors (GB.DES. 1977) said:

> Without exception the heads have qualities of imagination and vision, tempered by realism, which have enabled them to sum up not only their present situation but also attainable future goals'. (p.36).

Any attempt to sum up the characteristics of the head's role by considering both a selection of views of heads drawn from a number of European countries and a selection of the views of researchers working on both sides of the Atlantic, is rendered extremely difficult because of the complexity of the role which is recognized by all. Nevertheless, it may be possible to discern certain aspects of the role which are apparently common to the countries which are the subject of this study and which therefore may serve as a common basis when considering the training of heads for their job.

1. It would seem possible to draw up analyses of the tasks undertaken by heads and to list the *knowledge* and *skills* required to perform those tasks. There will inevitably be considerable variations in emphasis between different countries in this area, e.g. in certain countries a knowledge of law will be more important, in others curriculum matters may demand more attention. This

study of knowledge and skills may be particularly important to newly appointed heads but, on the other hand, certain knowledge may become necessary to all, including the most experienced heads at certain times, e.g. developments in technology or multi-cultural issues. Certain tasks and skills are general to all management situations and others are specific to educational institutions, e.g. all managers need skill in chairing meetings but heads require particular skills in the field of motivating adolescents and adults. Such basic skills and knowledge may be said to constitute an essential 'survival kit'.

2. Certain aspects of the head's role are inherent in the position or the *situation,* in which the individual head finds himself or herself. Performance and effectiveness in the role will depend upon the personality of the head in question and the awareness of self in that situation. It will also depend upon his or her sensitivity to others and ability to communicate, negotiate and mediate between sometimes conflicting individuals or groups, who are often exerting considerable pressure. Of increasing importance in the head's 'situation' are those influences and pressures which come from *outside* the school and for which an academic training and a career as a teacher do not prepare him or her. The demands for schools to be increasingly open to society and to respond to the conflicting demands of different members of society raise particular problems and demand particular skills in the field of communication, negotiation and 'marketing'. This area of the head's role is very *specific* to the individual school and to the individual community.

3. The third aspect of the role of the head which is becoming of increasing importance is the part which he or she plays in relation to educational *change*. Major changes in society which are taking place at this time are changing schools and are therefore changing the roles of heads who will find themselves responsible for these changes, sometimes in spite of themselves. This process requires qualities of leadership which involve imagination,

initiative, resource, creativity, vision and sound judgement—perhaps an element of risk-taking.

A number of different characterizations of the head's role have been used: benevolent autocrat, chief executive, leading professional, stabilizer and innovator. Others are in use, such as facilitator and orchestrator. We have talked of the 'helicopter pilot' and at the Windsor workshop Clive Hopes quoted Schmitz (1980) as complaining that 'The principal is no longer the leader of the school and no longer the captain of the ship, but merely the pilot or helmsman steering through the shallows and between rocks' (p. 88). Mats Ekholm and the Swedish team talk of the head's task of 'mapping' the development of the school as it edges its way into a very uncertain future. The diversity of these characterizations reveals the problem of attempting to catch the essentials of the head's role in a word or a phrase.

In summing up the Windsor workshop Seamus Hegarty as rapporteur expressed the problem thus:

It is not simply the case however that the school leader has multiple roles or even that the roles are changing. The most challenging feature in the present context is that the school leader's role is evolving from a situation of stable definition to one of emergent definition. It is not a question of moving from being a traditional head—benevolent despot or whatever—to another well-defined role as chief executive or leading professional. The school leader is moving into a situation where role definitions are to a degree continually evolving ... It means that school leaders cannot simply get down to doing their job. They have also constantly to be asking themselves what they *should* be doing. It is fair to say that most people find the former far easier. The 'frantic succession of disconnected activities' which characterizes the daily routine of many school leaders is indeed a defence against the painful task of self-analysis and role examination. How does one train people for emergent roles? Is it possible to provide training that will enable people to respond creatively to new situations? (Hegarty, 1983, pp. 134-5).

The role of the head which has been developed in the first part of this study is a changing role in the present and one which is likely to continue to change as schools change in the future. It has grown over the years in two dimensions.

First, the role has grown in terms of *space.* The area of concern of a head has increased and continues to spread beyond the confines of the school, which becomes more open and involved with society and with its individual community. Likewise the school is becoming increasingly influenced by that community and accountable to it. The head is Janus in this situation, acting as the gate-keeper who interprets the school to its community and vice versa. Secondly, the role is adding a dimension of *time,* as the head needs to become increasingly future orientated and responsible for resolving the 'present-future' dilemma for a school. This increased emphasis on the role of the head as an agent of change and also as a maintainer of stability heightens the tensions which are now implicit in the job and presents an interesting paradox to which, henceforth, the trainers will need to give increasing attention.

CHAPTER 2

The Training Needs of Heads

The first chapter of this study has considered the role of the head or principal of a secondary school as it is now and as it may evolve in the foreseeable future. We now turn our attention to examining what training may be necessary to perform that role effectively.

Certain general conclusions from the study of the head's role may serve as a starting point:

1. A head needs certain basic knowledge and skills preferably before taking up the appointment of head or at an early stage in his or her career as a head.

2. A head needs to be effective in a particular situation, i.e. in a particular school, in a particular local education authority or school district, in a particular country. This effectiveness will depend upon an awareness of self in that situation and sensitivity to that environment, particularly to other people with whom it is shared.

3. A head will need to give increasing attention to the future and to the development of the school into that future. This requires the development of skills in the leadership of a developing organization. Future developments for which particular training may be necessary are in the important areas of curriculum and organization. Curriculum change may become an increasing concern of the head and the development of a democratic school will certainly require the full involvement of the head.

Where there is a national initiative to provide training for the heads of schools the basic needs may be laid down centrally. This may be seen in the case of Sweden and of France, the countries which have the most highly developed training schemes for heads in Europe.

In the report of the SIA Commission (1974) which was concerned to examine and make recommendations on the inner working of the compulsory secondary school in Sweden, certain recommendations were made regarding the training needs of heads if these proposals were to be effective.

> Headmasters and directors of studies play a very important part in school activities. At present they lack the training required for many of the tasks which will be confronting them. SIA proposals are very much dependent for their realization on the ability of the school management to direct school activities in accordance with the guidelines contained in statutes and curricula. School management training is therefore very important and should include a wide range of practical and theoretical items. (p. 114).

Similarly, in the report of the Commission on 'Teacher Training' presided over by André de Peretti (1982) in France, Chapter 12 is devoted to the training of heads. Particular emphasis is laid on the evolution of the role:

> The job of the head has already undergone significant changes in recent years. It is very likely that it will be affected in the very near future by changes which can now be foreseen: decentralization and the increasing autonomy of the school. (de Peretti, p. 187).

There follow a series of proposals for further elaborating the national scheme for training heads which is already well developed:

> An initial training, centred more on aspects of relationships, on situational analysis and on participation in school management, will form a firm basis for defining new objectives and new content for the training of heads. (p.188).

In a centralized system of education one source for identifying the training needs may be such official documents which set out the objectives of the training which are to be taken up and developed by the trainers. However, in many countries no such guidelines exist and one must ask what other methods may be sought to identify training needs. Whose perception of needs are to be recognized and responded to by the trainers? There are the needs as perceived by the trainers and the needs of the trainees themselves. These different perspectives of need were examined by Hopes in his paper to the Gatwick conference (see ATEE and NAHT, 1982), against a background of experience of providing courses in the Federal Republic of Germany.

Trainers and trainees are placed in the dilemma of conflict of perceptions. We have the needs as perceived:

1. commonly by the trainers and trainees;
2. by the trainee only;
3. by the trainer only;
4. by neither the trainer nor trainee.

It is the responsibility of trainers to try and define these areas continuously. In the relatively new area of educational management it can be too easy for some trainers to move in with copious information, a cognitive input which does little to improve performance or contribute towards a more effective principalship. A scheme can only be justified when it can be shown that it is contributing towards the improvement of skills and competencies of participants.

Certainly, there is a heavy responsibility on those who organize training programmes to seek ways of learning about and understanding the needs of the clients. There are also grave dangers, which are expressed vividly by Hopes, if those with academic qualifications in management and organization 'come with a mission to enlighten those whom they perceive as ignorant, incompetent schoolmen, lost in the ramshackle world of education'.

Two possible approaches to examining training needs are,

firstly, for trainers to meet participants before they embark upon a training programme to discuss their needs with them or secondly to seek feedback from participants who have undergone a training programme to ascertain to what extent their needs have been met. The latter evaluation method certainly provides the trainers with valuable information but it is always retrospective and therefore of no help to the participant who has completed the programme. It is the writer's experience that there is much to be gained from visits paid to participants in their schools before a training programme begins. Such visits can allay fears, establish a relationship and provide valuable information for trainers on the particular needs of individuals. It is also valuable to meet a participant first in the more secure environment of his or her own school. Another process for identifying needs is to involve participants in the planning of all or of parts of the programme. To do this may involve gathering them together, a considerable time before the course begins. There is useful experience to be drawn on here from Norway, and from Northern Ireland.

In his paper to the Windsor workship (see Hegarty (Ed), 1983) Hopes refers to seminars held before the development of training schemes for the purposes of defining training needs:

> Frequently, the consequence of such seminars is a vast amount of information about the areas of activity of the principal in an 'ideal' form. The danger is that lists of needs can readily become categories for cognitive content, which are only helpful for the improvement of conceptual skills. They do not clarify the appropriate method for the training of skills. (p.90).

This implies that it is very useful to discuss with participants not only 'what' they wish to learn about during their training, but also 'how' they would wish to learn it. Such mature and experienced adults often have clear views on which methods of learning work for them. However, there are problems in seeking the needs directly from the participants themselves because sometimes expectations are raised which may not be satisfied for various reasons.

Hughes indicated another aspect of the problem at Windsor when referring to the work of Turner (1981) during a year's secondment from his headship. The perceptions of the participants and the course provider can be very different. He surveyed the views of 66 newly appointed first-time secondary heads in England by questionnaire and interview and found that they placed little reliance on 'concepts, techniques, theories or perspectives'.

> Turner concludes that there is a wide gap between the reliance of newly appointed heads on incidental, unstructured experience, inherent personal qualities and the example of colleagues and the belief of training course providers in the potential of planned, multi-dimensional but coherent programmes of preparation and training. (p.28).

There seems to be an expressed need particularly on the part of newly-appointed heads for information on such subjects as law, regulations and finance and also a need to engage in very specific problem-solving. These needs are genuinely felt and have been echoed in a number of the groups of heads met by the writer in different European countries. Course providers need to respond to such demands but not to rely entirely upon such topics in course or programme design. There is a danger, in the view of this writer, of courses degenerating into simply a sequence of 'practical tips' about how the system works, accompanied by lengthy descriptions by successful heads on how they run their schools.

A further problem in the area of identifying training needs is that of differentiating in training programmes to take account of individual needs and of different types of experience in the past. This has proved to be a problem which has grown in England with the increase in the number of management courses available not only for heads and for deputy heads but also for what has come to be called middle management. This includes heads of subject departments and staff with 'pastoral' responsibilities. Hopes emphasized at Windsor the importance of endeavouring to discover those tasks which heads had *not* performed before their appointment. He showed that in a sample of principals asked to estimate the percentage of their current tasks which they had already performed before taking over the principalship the largest group recorded 30 per cent of their present tasks and a substantial number recorded 100 per cent! Very often the participants are given 'standard' courses which in content and depth are undifferentiated. Sometimes, efforts are made to offer optional modules within a course or to provide alternative themes or topics according to type of school but generally programmes are provided with no consideration for individual needs because no real attempt to ascertain needs has been made. Further treatment of this problem will be found in the papers of Clive Hopes presented to the Gatwick Conference and to the Windsor workshop but the dilemma remains for trainers who are responsible for setting up training programmes. Whose needs are we trying to meet and if there is an 'ideal' against which to measure the 'training gap' to be filled, then who decides what the 'ideal' is? It is the writer's view that there is no simple solution to this problem and in his experience the most valuable source of advice came from practising heads who were invited to act as consultant course tutors while still performing their jobs. They usually served the centre for a period of about one year, participated in planning and acted as discussion group leaders during the courses or study-conferences. Their advice and help was invaluable in identifying current needs and over the years a substantial body of consultant expertise was built up in the region served by the Centre where the writer worked.

In spite of the difficulties faced by trainers when attempting to meet the training needs of heads, needs which we recognize are changing as the schools change and as the role of the head changes in consequence, the fact remains that it is necessary to seek some frameworks for planning training, given the very incomplete state of the art. A number of such frameworks have emerged from the seminars and conferences under review and may be helpful in that they are attempts to reach some European consensus.

From the discussions at Pont-à-Mousson (1982) four 'domains' were identified:

1. Pedagogic leadership: the curricular concerns of the head.

2. Administrative and financial management: the concern of the head for maintaining routines.
3. Human relationships both inside and outside the school.
4. Changes and renewal: the concerns of the head as motivator and change agent.

Emphasis was also placed on the increasing importance of 'team' management. The qualities seen as essential to a head were that he or she should be:

1. Open and available to the young, to their families and to the environment.
2. Flexible and adaptable: two permanent problems will be the evolution of the school system and the continual need to resolve conflicts.
3. Stable: to maintain the autonomy of the school, while respecting national laws and local regulations.

At Kristiansand (1982), the discussion groups were asked to indicate what they saw as the training needs of heads given the changing nature of the job. Their proposals included the following:

1. Human relationships: communication skills, motivating, problem-solving, group leadership, team-building.
2. Curriculum development: particularly in Sweden, Norway, Denmark, Austria and in the UK.
3. Self-management: self-awareness, handling stress, management of time.
4. Organization: setting up structures, setting targets, evaluating outcomes.
5. Entrepreneurial skills: negotiation inside and outside school, promoting the interests of the school.
6. Managing innovation: planning and implementing change, awareness of social, economic and political trends in society, awareness of the new technology —vision.
7. Effective leadership skills.

A further list of professional development needs related to

the effective school headship arose from group discussions at the European Forum on Educational Administration: Intervisitation Programme in the Federal Republic of Germany 1980. (Report edited by Clive Hopes). The order in which the items appear has no significance.

1. Personnel management
— planning
— recruitment
— development
— appraisal
— experience in teachers' in-service training
— management of professional and non-professional staff

2. Interpersonal skills
— communicating
— motivating
— counselling
— handling conflict
— committees and chairmanship
— group behaviour
— group leadership

3. Self-management
— managing stress
— management of one's own time
— self-awareness
— self-development

4. Institutional planning
— assessing information from within and outside the school
— forecasting trends and needs
— determining policies and priorities
— institutional evaluation (organizing, reporting results, discussing results)
— determining policies, goals and values

5. Resource management
- estimating
- budgetary control
- financial management

6. Curriculum skills
- development of curriculum
- management of curriculum

7. Management of innovation
- creating innovations
- reacting to innovations
- responding to innovations
- implementing

8. Organizational skills
- devising internal management structures
- devising academic structures and record systems
- allocating duties and tasks
- understanding the school as an organization

9. Relating to governmental systems
- reporting to regulatory system
- reporting to regional, state, national system
- negotiating: with regulatory system
            with other authorities
- experience in the administration

10. Relating to the local environment
- community
- public relations
- relation to professional groups
- parents
- church
- local industry
- culture
- press
- politicians

11. Knowledge of laws
- law in relation to school
- personal rights
- youth and social laws

12. Educational leadership
- supervision
- advising
- methodology
- discipline
- school events

13. Relating to pupils/students
- dealing with individuals and groups
- dealing with seriously disruptive
- dealing with seriously disturbed

14. School as a system in relation to other environmental systems
- system analysis

15. Developing a philosophy of headship
- role of the head
- styles of leadership
- awareness of values in relation to managing
- approaches to managing (Annex A5–A6)

These lists are useful in that they represent the combined thinking of practising heads, of trainers and of educational administrators from a number of European countries. They define broad 'areas' in which training is needed but owing to the time limitations of international gatherings do not go into great detail, particularly about the nature of the learning involved and about the methods of learning which may be appropriate. Such analysis of needs may be likened to the attempts that have been made in some individual countries to build a task or skill profile of the head's job. An example of such a task analysis was given in Chapter 1 of Morgan and Hall's report of the POST project in England (1982), in which three of the four clusters were derived from the classification of administrative skills by Katz (1974): technical skills, conceptual skills and human skills, to which Morgan and Hall add a fourth category of 'external management'.

Glatter in his paper to the Windsor workshop (in Hegarty (Ed), 1983) illustrated several attempts to build frameworks of skills categories. An ambitious attempt to define these for assessment purposes in a USA context forms the basis of the Assessment Centre package of the National Association of Secondary School Principals (NASSP). Twelve skill dimensions to be assessed were derived from official job descriptions and from interviews with people having a close knowledge of the job (Morgan 1981). These skill dimensions were used as a basis for the construction of a set of situational exercises and a structured guide for assessment interviews. The twelve dimensions (to which definitions were attached) are:

1. problem analysis	7. stress tolerance
2. judgement	8. oral communication
3. organizational ability	9. written communication
4. decisiveness	10. range of interests
5. leadership	11. personal motivation
6. sensitivity	12. educational values

It must be stressed that this list of skill dimensions is intended primarily for the purposes of assessment which may be used by educational authorities when selecting for principalship posts but, as Glatter points out, it contains recommendations for further training and development activities and an individual can use it as a diagnostic aid to help rectify weaknesses or improve abilities. The scheme is currently being validated at Michigan State University. This work clearly has implications for training and for trainers and illustrates again how difficult it is to meet individual needs because heads or potential heads do not start work with a 'clean sheet' but come with a variety of experience, skills and backgrounds. Consequently, however structured courses may be, most training will be additive or compensatory. Furthermore, the responsibility of the individual head for his or her own development may be a significant factor in the progress of that development. Glatter refers to the recent movement towards 'self-development'

(Burgoyne *et al.* 1978), which is justified on psychological grounds: that learning will be more effective and motivation greater if the content and method is selected and controlled largely by the learner in accordance with his or her own perceptions of needs and interests: the individual will tend to 'own' the learning to a greater extent than if it is specified from above.

There is an evident degree of consensus to be found in these various analyses and the checklists have a value both for heads themselves and for those who are responsible for providing training programmes for heads at national, regional or local level. Their main value, in the view of the writer, lies in the extent to which they clarify or illuminate the job which is one beset with much confusion, subject to a multitude of pressures and 'often a frantic succession of disconnected activities'.

The most commonly identified 'areas' in which there is a need for training appear to be the following:

1. Managing oneself, e.g. self-awareness, self-development, managing stress, managing time

2. Managing people, e.g. recruitment, staff development, assessment, communication, motivation, handling conflict, negotiation, mediation, chairmanship, group behaviour, counselling

3. Managing the curriculum, e.g. curriculum appraisal, curriculum planning and development, priorities and balance, monitoring classroom performance

4. Managing resources, e.g. managing plant and equipment, budgetary control, financial management

5. Managing the organization, e.g. setting up and maintaining

	structures for consultation, devising systems for record-keeping and documentation, delegating duties and tasks, routine management
6. Managing change and development,	e.g. long-term strategy and planning, overview, scenario building, creating innovation, responding to demands for innovation, implementing changes
7. Managing external relations,	e.g. relating to the national, regional or state system, relating to parents, employers, politicians, the press, the local community, etc.
8. Leadership,	e.g. the contemporary role of the head in a developing democratic school. Leadership styles
9. Knowledge of law,	e.g. the law relating to schools and to young people.

The sub-headings are not intended to be comprehensive but to serve as examples of the tasks, activities, knowledge or skills for which some training may be needed. Clearly there are overlaps between the different 'areas' and, for example, leadership could appear as an aspect of the management of people. It appears separately because it is a singularly important aspect of the role of the head and one for which training is particularly needed.

One or two comments can be offered concerning the value of such analyses and of which a summary has been attempted. Firstly, one must emphasize the vast range of knowledge and skills that is implied by such lists, however brief they may appear in a summary. Secondly, they indicate, by implication, the extent of the training programmes required if these needs are to be met in any depth. We are made conscious of only being at the very beginning of the process of providing a training which is adequate or appropriate for the size or importance of the job. A further value of such analyses is to reveal how little of the job can be simply acquired in a cognitive form from lecturers or from books. If we consider the skills implied in the first two categories listed above, namely managing oneself and managing people, comparatively little can be learned about either in any depth and then internalized without interaction with other people. The techniques of teaching and learning about interpersonal skills remain notoriously complex and time-consuming. Knowledge of law remains perhaps one of the few areas where a straightforward cognitive input by lecture is much valued by heads and considered to be very supportive. A large proportion of the learning which relates to people, to organization, to consultation, to decision-making, to managing change and development and to leadership seems to lie in the field of acquiring skills in practice rather than in the acquiring of knowledge. Mintzberg (1975) expresses clearly this challenge to the trainers of managers:

> Cognitive learning is detached and informational, like reading a book or listening to a lecture. It is necessary but cognitive learning no more makes a manager than it does a swimmer. The latter will drown the first time he jumps into the water, if the coach never takes him out of the lecture hall, gets him wet, and gives him feedback on his performance. (p.61).

The particular skills which Mintzberg mentions as requiring this type of training are (a) peer relationships (b) carrying out negotiations (c) motivating subordinates (d) resolving conflicts (e) establishing information networks and disseminating information (f) making decisions in conditions of extreme ambiguity (g) allocating resources, and (h) introspective skills about himself and his job. (p. 61). The skills he mentions are very similar to those which appear in the various lists of skills which are considered necessary to be an effective head.

This brief consideration of some of the training implications of the list of needs which has been compiled from a fairly wide range of sources suggests that a variety of problems face those who have a responsibility to provide such training. Before proceeding, it may be helpful to draw some conclusions which seem to follow from this chapter. These conclusions represent a personal view.

1. The range of knowledge, skills and attitudes needed to be an effective head is very wide.

2. Each of the 'areas' of need included could be studied in varying degrees of depth and at various stages in the head's career.

3. While some of the 'areas' or some aspects of individual 'areas' of need may have figured in the previous professional training of heads, a substantial proportion of these 'areas' will not have been encountered before.

4. Heads, on appointment, will have a wide variety of previous experience and background. Consequently, their individual training needs will vary considerably.

5. While there are a number of perspectives of what the appropriate needs are in particular cases, e.g. those of national or local educational systems, those of the trainers and those of the heads themselves, priority should be given when devising schemes of training to those needs which are expressed by heads themselves.

6. While certain examples of the 'areas' of need may be satisfied by cognitive learning, a very considerable proportion of the skills involved, particularly those skills concerning relations with people, will only be learned effectively in practical situations.

7. If a head is to be helped to perform effectively within a specific school situation, a significant proportion of any training programme needs to be related to his or her own school and its environment and may need to take place within that environment.

CHAPTER 3

How Training Needs are Being Met

It is the purpose of this part of the study to examine the ways in which certain training needs are being met in some European countries. Given the constraints of the study and the very rapid expansion of training in school management in certain European countries, such an examination is inevitably very selective and very partial.

On the opening day of the Windsor workshop Ian Butterworth, HMI, in welcoming members on behalf of the Department of Education and Science drew the important distinction between the enduring skills of leadership and the management of change. The former is concerned with how well the individual is being equipped with the knowledge and skills necessary to be an effective leader, whereas the latter asks less about the person being trained and more about the institution for which he or she is responsible. This distinction expresses the broad difference in approaches to training heads which may be seen in the European countries visited during this study.

In the short period that formal training programmes have existed in Western Europe two traditions have developed; one is mainly concerned with training individuals and the other is primarily concerned with improving schools. In the view of the writer a third tradition is emerging which is concerned with achieving both these objectives by the adoption of an approach to training which combines both processes. Consequently for this study case studies of training programmes have been selected which illustrate these three approaches in the belief that they represent the most significant trends which may be seen in Europe at present.

The first two examples illustrate clearly the distinction between the two main traditions and they also represent the two most highly developed national programmes in Europe. These are drawn from France and from Sweden. The French programme is aimed at training individuals for their jobs. The Swedish programme, while training individuals, is mainly aimed at developing their schools.

A further example of a programme aimed mainly at individual development is taken from England and has been developed at a regional centre.

The last two case studies are of programmes which claim to be concerned with the development of both individuals and of schools. These examples are drawn from the Netherlands and from Norway and are distinguished by being of very different duration. The selection represents a broad range of emphasis rather than sharp exclusive distinctions. There are clearly considerable areas of overlap between the programmes chosen and, for example, the training programmes in Sweden, while being focused mainly on school development, would claim to involve individual development, and those programmes in the UK which are mainly concerned with individual development do not ignore the issues of school development. However, there is, in the view of the writer, a significant difference in emphasis between those training schemes which originate from an in-service training tradition of individual development and those which have emerged from a tradition of organizational development.

France

In France the programme is impressive because of its logical development of an initial training programme for all newly-appointed school leaders which is now well established and also because of the continuity of the training which is now envisaged. Follow-up training to the initial programme is now accepted for the first year of experience as a head and continued in-service training is now proposed at regular intervals. There are further proposals to increase the present initial training from three months to one year.

The necessity to provide training programmes arose from the

events of 1968. The gradual devolution of powers and responsibilities since 1972 from the Ministry to the *Académies,* or regional bodies with responsibilities for education, has led in turn to a greater demand for devolution of powers to the schools. All these changes and others have rendered the role of the principal in France far more complex and as a result training for future heads and deputies became obligatory in 1971. Originally, the training took the form of a ten-day seminar. Then in 1973 a Circular was issued from the Ministry which laid down the guidelines upon which future training would be based. Some of those guidelines were as follows.

1. The training would be for all newly-appointed heads.
2. Training would be for a period of three months during the third term of the school year.
3. Training would be full-time and participants would be relieved of all other duties during the period of training.
4. The programme would be coordinated nationally but would be essentially regional in character.
5. Training teams would be established in each *Académie.*
6. There would be emphasis on flexibility in the approach and diversity was anticipated.
7. The roles of the teacher and the head were very different and every effort would be made to alert the new principal to his new responsibilities and in particular to the importance of human relationships.
8. The formal period of training would be inadequate and incomplete. It would need to be followed up by in-service training.
9. Participants would spend part of the training, about two weeks, in a commercial concern or in an administrative organization not associated with education.
10. Contacts with employers, with professional organizations and with the social services would be encouraged.
11. The methods used would involve alternating periods spent in schools with periods at their training centres, thus linking learning with practice.
12. At the end of the period of training participants might spend several days in the school to which they had been appointed.

13. The training would be evaluated by the participants.
14. Apart from these general guidelines, freedom is given to the training teams to determine the time to be spent in different activities, the content and the training methods. Participants will be encouraged to express their own needs.

This circular was a significant document in that it illustrates the value of national guidelines, which delegated responsibility to regional bodies and encouraged flexibility. In fact the word *souplesse* appears in many subsequent documents relating to the training. Also the important principle of enlarging the sphere of interest of the school leaders was clearly established as well as the value of a practical approach involving many visits, much observation and subsequent reflection. The delegation of the training to regions was also an important step and Claude Caré speaking about the programme at Pont-à-Mousson, 1982, said that it was the first example of effective decentralization in the French education system.

The training began in 1974 and while there has been continuous evaluation by the trainees and the trainers and some diversity in content and method in the various *Académies*, the basic format has met with general approval and has not been changed to any great extent.

A further Circular issued in 1981 has introduced a number of significant modifications to the original guidelines which are as follows:

1. Initial training is only the first step in the total career development of a school leader. In-service training is an equally necessary part of that development.
2. Initial training would have two phases:
   (a) the course prior to taking up appointment, and
   (b) the training during the first year of appointment.
3. The preparatory course would last for a minimum period of eleven weeks and would include:
   (a) four weeks in a school.
   (b) five weeks with the training team.
   (c) two weeks in a commercial firm.

4. The school in which a participant spent time would be of a similar type to that in which he or she was going to work as a school leader.

5. The periods spent with the training teams would aim at giving the participants the minimum essential skills necessary to take up their appointments and the training would be based on the direct experience of participants during the periods in schools.

6. The first year in an appointment would be a probationary year. The school leader would be put in touch with a neighbouring head upon whom he or she could call.

7. During the second term of the first year the school leaders would be brought together for brief periods with the training teams who would take account of their expressed needs following upon their experience in the job.

8. In addition to further in-service training days devoted to particular topics, the heads in a particular district would meet together each term to discuss matters which they proposed.

This document represents an evolution of the training programme which:

1. introduces the notion of a total planned career development for school leaders, to include initial training and in-service training;

2. extends the initial training to include a probationary first year, subject to inspection and involving further training;

3. introduces the notion of linking a newly-appointed school leader with an experienced neighbour;

4. and introduces the idea of regular meetings of heads in a district for mutual support.

In addition to these developments, there is a reinforced emphasis on a practical and problem-solving approach as a method of training.

Further developments in the evolution of the training

programme can be anticipated in France. M. Vergnaud, the *Directeur des Collèges,* in opening the seminar at Pont-à-Mousson referred to the training of school leaders as an integral part of the reforms now being proposed as a result of two important Commissions which have reported recently. These are the Commissions chaired by André de Peretti and by Professor Louis Legrand. The first of these deals with teacher training and includes an evaluation of the existing programme of training school leaders and proposals for its future development.

The training of school leaders in France is a decentralized activity in what is still recognized as a centralized system of education and so before turning to look in more detail at the initial training at regional level, it may be worth considering the organization at national level. The central training agency is the *Service de la Formation Administrative* (SFA) which has eight directorates, one of which has a responsibility for providing training for the members of the regional training teams. The headquarters team comprises four full-time members of staff, including one head of a school on a four-year secondment, a university professor and a training methods specialist. The task of the team is to provide training for about 600 voluntary trainers in the 27 *Académies.*

The SFA team provides support in the form of

1. a documentation service, including training materials such as case studies
2. three-day training courses: each year courses are run for half the training teams who send two or three trainers to take part. They then return to their teams to pass on their training. The training is concerned mainly with methods, particularly group dynamics, and course construction but also each year deals with major themes which may be appropriate as the basis for work within the programmes of regional teams. Examples of such themes are: human relations, the management of finance, community involvement, the conduct of meetings.

At regional level the body responsible for the selection of

trainers and for the organization of training programmes is the *Equipe académique d'animation de la vie scolaire.* Some of the *Académies* are now combined because of the smaller numbers to be trained and in the year 1980–81 there were 15 training teams. An *Inspecteur d'Académie* is in charge of each team of trainers who are selected for their personal qualities and ability in the teaching of adults. The team may include heads, deputies, bursars, administrative personnel and teachers but heads are in the majority. The teams vary in size considerably and the *Académies* clearly need teams of different sizes to meet local circumstances. M. Toussaint reporting on the work of the teams over the period from 1971–77 observed that the aim was to involve as many trainers as possible in order to spread the load. However, this creates some difficulties in course continuity. The growth in the total number of trainers and the need to replace or relieve existing trainers has led to considerable turnover—three teams having been completely replaced during the period under review. Trainers are volunteers, receive no payment and are granted little remission from their normal duties. Nevertheless, there is evident enthusiasm for the task which is seen by many as a form of personal career development. Very few give up the job as trainers because they wish to. Toussaint also describes a wide variety of organizational patterns which are adopted within the guidelines provided and *Académies* are still trying to find the best structure for their teams.

Derek Esp reported on the strengths and weaknesses of the training teams following his visits in 1980.

It is a strong point of the French system that full-time trainers are deployed on the key tasks of training and supporting an enthusiastic army of volunteers. This can bring problems, however. Selection of the volunteer trainers is left to the *Inspecteurs d'Académie,* some of whom have good experience of training schemes. Others may only have a vague understanding of the requirements and objectives of the scheme. Again, support from the centre depends on a pyramid structure and this can have weak links. Some *Académies* are fortunate to be self-sufficient in terms of experienced trainers who can train and select the local team. Others have such problems of staff turnover that a viable team of trainers is difficult to sustain. (Esp, 1981, p.19).

Before turning our attention to the initial courses themselves two points need to be made. Firstly, initial training of school leaders in France, although not directly related to the selection process, is linked to it. Selection of school leaders takes place annually by a national process, which culminates in the publication of a *liste d'aptitude* of those who may be appointed to posts as school leaders for the following year. More candidates are nominated always than are actually needed. This lengthy process of selection takes place between November and April. Then during the third or summer term all those who have been nominated receive the initial training. There are two forms of initial training: the long course, which has already been outlined, comprising eleven weeks' training and which is followed by all those who have previously been teachers or a short course of ten days' training for those who have previous administrative experience as, e.g. deputy heads. This distinction between the two types of courses is a source of some resentment among deputies and may well be changed in the future to give greater equality of training and in order to create coherence in school management teams. The second point that needs to be made is that the potential candidates have received little or no preparation for an administrative post if they have been teachers because there is no system of 'middle management' appointments such as that which exists, for example, in the UK. Initial training, therefore, upon or before appointment is seen as particularly essential.

It is worth noting the size of this training programme. 2,000 people were trained on the long and short courses in 1976, 1,200 in 1980 and in 1982, 1,109. Of that last number, the percentage of course members who obtained appointments was, in the case of the long courses, 55 per cent and in the case of the short courses 59 per cent.

Examples of Initial Training Programmes

There follows some further information about two initial

training programmes, both for the year 1981–82. One is taken from the *Académie* of Lille and the other from the joint *Académies* of Dijon and Besançon. The writer is particularly indebted for documentation, for advice and for personal help in studying these programmes to M. Claude Caré, *Inspecteur d'Académie* (Besancon-Dijon), to M. R. Wattiaux, *Inspecteur d'Académie* (Lille) and to heads, deputies and trainers who took part in the training programmes.

In Lille, there were 29 members of the long course and 44 following the short course. The *Inspecteur d'Académie* in charge preferred a large training team from which to select teams to look after particular sessions. He stressed the importance of good group leaders for discussion sessions. The qualities required were sensitivity and a capacity to create honesty and confidence in others. He saw the training role as part of the staff development of his heads. A large team enabled him to renew his teams continually and give experience as trainers to many. He claimed to have some 70 people on whom he could call to compose a training team for a course of 30.

The long course took place during 12 weeks from April to June 1982. The first week is always an induction period looked after by a very respected and experienced head who takes the group on a series of visits of different types of educational institutions to give members some impression of the scope of an educational system. He seeks to establish the coherence of the group and to introduce group methods of working which will be used during the course.

Six weeks were spent with the training team. Two periods of two weeks were spent in a school similar to the one they were going to work in. There were also two weeks spent in a commercial concern. For each week spent with the training team there was a theme and one week was spent in residence. A number of different centres were used for the various sessions and a teachers' training college for the week in residence (a hotel would be inappropriate and expensive in the view of the *Inspecteur d'Académie)*. During these weeks there were other visits to educational institutions related to the themes and followed by discussions. Other individuals encountered came from the social services, from the business world and from the administration. The teaching methods used were lectures followed by discussion, work in groups, video recordings, closed-circuit television and role play. The *Inspecteur d'Académie* said that there was always the danger of too much theory. Heads are, above all, practitioners and he advocated a very practical approach to the training: 'Theory is only for reflection, not for taking refuge behind'. There was a three-hour session at the end of each week devoted to evaluation of that week's work and a final evaluation at the end of the course.

A group of heads who had been through the course strongly supported the idea that some training was necessary and emphasized the loneliness of the job and the increased pressures under which they were working. Becoming a head was a great change and indeed something of a shock after being a teacher. They appreciated much that the course had tried to do for them in raising the awareness of what to expect. As one put it 'I was given an idea of what I was to expect and became more humble'. Their major problem was that they had not yet had the experiences against which to set what they were learning: 'We had no questions because we had not lived the life of a principal'.

Some valued the opportunity to sit back and think away from a school, others valued help in sorting out some of the priorities. There was general agreement that skill in personal relationships could not be taught in the abstract and they did not think role play was very successful. An experienced head who was at the same meeting thought the 12-week course was a considerable step forward. She considered that the practical part of the training, on the job, did not last long enough, whereas the theoretical side offered such a tremendous amount of data that it was not realistic to believe that it could all be assimilated. The 1982 course included, for the first time, the study of such essential subjects as the conduct of meetings and speaking in public. This initiative should be encouraged. It ought to pave the way to a true psychological training and offer heads a serious course in sensitization to group phenomena which would help them in the conduct of meetings, in negotiating with different groups and individuals and in resolving conflict.

51

In the *Académie* of Besançon-Dijon the long course during the year 1982 was organized by the Académie of Dijon. The training team was smaller than that in Lille, numbering some 30 members, of whom 14 were heads. A document giving guidance to the trainers included the following advice:

1. Avoid a proliferation of themes which are dealt with in a fragmented way and become diffuse.
2. Allow some half-days following the third week of the course to be organized and conducted by the participants themselves.
3. Take care to avoid breaks in the rhythm of the training.
4. Include an evening entertainment once each residential week to prevent the group dispersing.
5. Maintain a balance between the collective activities of the group and the personal autonomy of the individual.
6. Encourage the participation of course members in daily evaluation, in organizing half-day sessions and in contributing their particular expertise to course sessions.

A detailed brief is given regarding the contributions of lecturers, including the following:

1. Avoid too frequent recourse to those in senior positions in the educational hierarchy.
2. Avoid lectures from 'specialists' unless their teaching ability is guaranteed.
3. Encourage contacts with personalities from outside the field of education who will present another perspective of that world.

Advice is given to chairpersons and to group leaders, e.g:

1. to be sensitive to the problem of outside lecturers coming in to a group which is already constituted, has wide experience and is highly critical
2. to be constantly on the alert to rescue sessions which are failing and to adapt to situations which are unforeseen: 'In all cases the lancet is more effective than the painkiller'.

All the course sessions are clearly very carefully prepared by this training team and the fullest documentation provided for the course members. One of the documents issued before the course to all participants attempts to capture the spirit of the training and of the methods to be used. Here are some examples of the principles suggested.

1. Only those who are themselves responsible can train those who are to become responsible. It is not a matter of exalted specialists. The training offered starts with practical experience and keeps returning to it.
2. We are addressing ourselves to intelligent people who can read. We shall not spend time developing what is written elsewhere. The collated work on Laws and Regulations (RLR) measure 1·8 metres long on a shelf. That is more than Balzac's *Comédie Humaine*. You would be better off reading Balzac!
3. Selection is the first process in training. An impossible course member always becomes an impossible school leader. The trainers assume that they have before them people who are alive, open, who enjoy exchanges and who have distinct personalities. A course does not provide character. It teaches you to accept your own self-image.
4. A group of course members between them know 90 per cent of what they are required to know. The training enables information to circulate among the group. A good trainer manages to get out of a group what each member of the group has to offer.
5. A training course must raise the level of confidence but maintain a level of disquiet. Anxieties about preparing a budget, making a timetable or conducting a meeting will be dealt with during the course. A level of anxiety, however, must be maintained because the real problems lie elsewhere. There is not always an administrative solution. In ten years, the job of a school leaver will have changed more than it has evolved since 1945. Technical knowledge acquired on this course will have a limited future use.
6. The most essential and the most difficult area is that of human relationships. The only serious difficulties and

the only conflicts which can get worse are those originating in relationships.

The style of leadership which characterized this initial training course was positive and dynamic but showed a respect for the experience and maturity of the participants and a concern that they should form a coherent group who participated in planning their own learning and evaluated their trainers rigorously. An *Inspecteur d'Académie* assured continuity throughout the whole course and a head was responsible for the detailed arrangements for the weeks spent with the training team.

There is an interesting contrast between the format of this long course and that in the *Académie* of Lille. In this case the arrangement of the weeks was as follows:

Week No. 1: two days of introduction to the course, three days in a school.
Week No. 2: spent in a school.
Week No. 3: spent in a commercial concern.
Week No. 4: spent with the training team.
Week No. 5: spent in a commercial concern.
Weeks No. 6, 7: spent with the training team.
Week No. 8: spent in a school.
Week No. 9: spent with the training team.
Week No. 10: spent in a school.
Week No. 11: spent with the training team.

There were 13 school leaders participating in this course, five from the *Académie* of Dijon and eight from the *Académie* of Besançon.

Features of the programme which are characteristic of the approach to training in this *Académie* are the following.

1. The initial two-day meeting, which included welcomes and an introduction to the course. The details of the programme were presented and the practical experience prepared for. It was a social occasion too.
2. Two periods of practical experience followed, seven days in a school and five days in a commercial concern.

54

3. The first week which was spent with the training team began with three days dealing with sensitivity training and with human relationships. There were 16 sessions of 90 minutes on this theme, dealing with oneself and others, the influences of attitudes and roles, and relationships both in and out of school. A number of the sessions were practical and involved case studies, discussion, observation and role play in front of TV cameras. Exercises included making a presentation, conducting a meeting and conducting an interview. The experiences of course members during the previous two weeks were drawn upon as a basis for discussion.

4. The participants experienced two 'other forms of training': they attended a session of an orchestra in rehearsal and were also addressed by a commandant in charge of army training. These experiences were intended to illustrate other styles of leadership and other forms of training and were aimed at training by analogy.

5. Two and a half days spread throughout the programme were devoted to themes chosen by the course members themselves.

6. There was continuous evaluation of each session by the course members and the final afternoon of each week spent with the training team was devoted to evaluation of the week. The final day of the course was also spent in evaluation. A summary of the course evaluation was published later with lessons to be borne in mind when planning the following year's programme.

This initial training programme was notable for the meticulous care with which the details of the course were prepared and for the amount of time which was devoted to that preparation. To quote the conclusion of the summary evaluation,

The preparation of the course necessitated 12 meetings of the training teams of the two *Académies*. During the preparatory period:
trainers travelled 21,110 kilometres,
they spent 268 hours travelling,

they devoted 720 hours to meetings and to preparation.
During the course itself:
trainers travelled 21,080 kilometres,
they spent 390 hours travelling,
they devoted 880 hours to the training and they spent 47
nights away from home.
In all, the course required:
more than 42,000 kilometres of travelling,
more than 660 hours on the road,
more than 1600 hours' work.

Evaluation of the initial training programmes in France at national level

The *Service de la Formation Administrative* in Paris, which is responsible for the coordination of the training programmes in France and for training the trainers, receives from each *Académie* the summaries of the evaluations which have been undertaken by course members and by trainers. A summary of all these evaluations is then produced, published and circulated to all *Académies* as a means of sharing the experiences of all.

The future of the initial training programme for school leaders in France

The present programmes of training have been developed over a period of nine years to a high level of sophistication. Nevertheless, it is probable that the programme will continue to evolve further, assuming that adequate resources can be found to expand the present provision. A consideration of the issues involved in equipping school leaders for their present but more particularly for their future responsibilities is to be found in the report of the Commission chaired by André de Peretti which examined both the initial and in-service training of teachers (de Peretti, 1982).

The report offers an evaluation of the present programme of initial training (pp. 73-75) and sets out a number of propositions for improving the training in the future (pp. 187–191).

The report comments first on the problems for trainers of a programme which takes place in the third term of the school year when schools and school leaders are already under particular pressure. The courses tend to have no recognized centres but to be itinerant, depending upon the willingness of institutions to accommodate them. The trainers are practitioners performing a training role part-time. While the training teams bring together people from all parts of the education system, there is a preponderance of heads and the teachers are insufficiently represented. Their training by the SFA *(Service de la Formation Administrative)* is mainly in methods of teaching.

The report comments favourably on the aims and intentions of the training but has reservations about the success with which aims are put into practice. The techniques acquired by trainers are not always mastered. There is a need for operational aims to be more precisely defined. The major criticism of the training concerns the issue of theory and practice. The training often deals with 'preoccupations which are too utilitarian and not sufficiently enriched by conceptual approaches and theoretical references'. The training needs to make further progress and gain 'a second wind' by a 'theoretical enrichment' of its contents and of its evaluation methods which are insufficiently concerned with formative auto-evaluation. The report recognizes that 'the training, such as it is, is well appreciated by the course members. It is effective in making school leaders rapidly operational'. It is seen by the Commission as providing a valuable point of departure for constructing 'a training adapted to the changes which are taking place in the French education system'.

Accordingly, the report goes on to make a number of propositions about the form of training for school leaders which would be appropriate in the future:

1. The changes in the role of the school leader which are foreseen include an increased emphasis upon the importance of relationships, in particular the dialogue with the users and the abilities to listen, to enter into dialogue, to negotiate and to convince. The increased autonomy of the school will mean a greater need to analyse the situation in which the school finds itself.

2. There will be a need to accentuate in training programmes this aspect of human relationships. Selection processes are important and people who are not capable of making relationships should not be selected. The 'whole person' must be a constant concern and each course session should be a subject for analysing the functioning of the group. Common themes should be self-awareness, relationship with groups, conduct of meetings, relationships with individuals and techniques of communication. Development of relationships must underpin the whole training in leadership.

3. There will be a need to increase the capacity of school leaders for situational analysis, notably of the school's environment. This implies being open to influences and sensitive to a network of relationships: 'School cannot live on the edge of its social and economic environment'. To undertake this analysis, knowledge and techniques are necessary. Theory needs to alternate with practice 'on the ground'.

4. There will be a need to improve the application of the principles of the training and to define operational aims. The theoretical level of inputs needs to be raised and better links established between theory and practice.

5. A common training for newly-appointed heads and former deputies will need to be established thus doing away with short courses and reinforcing the coherence of management teams.

6. The length of training should be increased to one year. This raises the question of the increased demands on trainers. Each trainee would be in a school to live through the most difficult times of the school year. The periods with the training teams would be spread over the whole year.

7. Each trainee would undertake a personal or collective project based on individual needs worked out at the beginning of the year with the trainers.

8. There will be a need to deepen the study of themes which are at present dealt with superficially. The following topics, for example, would benefit from in-depth study: situational analysis, adolescent psychology, the socio-

psychology of groups, adult learning, comparative studies and formative evaluation.

9. A plan of in-service training would need to be developed for those already in posts, and who had not benefited from the full training. In-service training would also be compulsory for school leaders for two weeks every year.

10. One year of sabbatical leave would be envisaged every six or seven years.

The forms of training which are foreseen by these far-reaching proposals may not come into being in the immediate future but nevertheless would raise the role of the school leader to a new level of professionalism. The appropriate training for such a role in the future is seen to comprise both initial and in-service training, and also to imply the development of a 'theory of practice' established on a firm conceptual base and a methodology of learning which is grounded in theories of adult learning.

Professor Louis Legrand, who was Chairman of the other Commission which reported to the Minister in 1983, making a further set of far-reaching proposals concerning the future of French schools, in an interview with the writer summed up the implications of his proposals for the training of school leaders as follows:

1. The role of a school leader of an autonomous democratic school closely involved with its local community is a very difficult one.

2. Selection is crucial because little can be done to change character and personality. A capacity to build good relationships is essential.

3. School leaders will need to be change agents and not simply people who apply regulations.

4. At present there is a lack of appropriate institutions for the training of school leaders.

5. There is also a lack of adequate learning theory in this field.

6. There will be a need to establish permanent and temporary posts as trainers.

7. Methodology must spring from the needs of the school leaders. Theory must respond to their questions and to their expressed concerns.
8. The duration of the training is too short to deal in depth with the training required by school leaders.
9. The isolation of school leaders is a major problem. They need to be brought together at regular intervals, perhaps every 15 days to share problems and to seek help if necessary.
10. A creator, not a conformist, is required in the role of school leader.

The programme which has been developed in France to train principals and senior staff is a very impressive one. The programme was initiated and is coordinated at the national level but has developed very flexibly at regional level, using, for the most part, volunteer trainers. The scheme has begun logically with the provision of initial training and is now being planned to provide continuous support for heads throughout their careers. Other countries have much to learn from the French experience.

Sweden

The second case study selected is that of Sweden. The example has been chosen because, as in the case of France, the training programme is highly developed and is organized on a national level. In contrast to the French programme, however, which provides primarily initial training, the scheme in operation in Sweden brings together school leaders of different ages and with varied experience quite deliberately. The term 'school leader' will be used throughout this section on Sweden because it is the term used by the Swedes themselves in descriptions of their own programmes, when translated into English. The term refers to heads, to deputy heads and to school directors, all of whom are involved in the training programme. A school director is the chief administrative officer responsible for the schools in a Swedish community.

A significant feature of the school leader training programme in Sweden is the extent to which it has been fully documented. The aims of the programme have been set out in a number of documents, there exist a number of accounts of the training, written by those involved in the training and by independent foreign observers, and also more has been done in Sweden to evaluate the programme than in any other European country. Recent accounts of the programme were given by those responsible at national level, Mats Ekholm and Eskil Stegö, to the seminar at Donaueschingen, to the Gatwick Conference and to the Windsor Workshop. All these documents, as well as the experience of a number of visits paid by the writer to Sweden, will be drawn upon in this section of the study.

The programme for training school leaders in Sweden cannot be fully appreciated without some reference to recent educational developments in that country because the programme is very much a part of those developments.

Recent educational developments in Sweden

Education has always been a central political issue in Sweden, a country which has a strong tradition of centralization. In the period of its existence, which is little more than 100 years, the school system has undergone a succession of reforms to raise the level of education of the people and also to bring about greater social equality. This climate of reform continues to be felt in Sweden and a former secondary head, now a school director, told the writer, 'We have been reformed all our lives as teachers'.

During a long and economically stable period, the social democratic party dominated political life and a comprehensive system of education was developed. In 1962, the compulsory nine-year comprehensive school for pupils aged seven to 16 was introduced and became fully operative in 1973. The first comprehensive curriculum was introduced in 1962 and has been significantly revised in 1969 and 1980. The most recent revision provides for a greater degree of autonomy for school leaders and for teachers. Under the old curriculum teachers were required to implement a detailed set of instructions. Now under the new curriculum they are offered policy statements, a rationale for the curriculum and guidelines about teaching it, but are expected to work out to a large extent the details of content and of method themselves. Responsibility has been pushed back to schools, to school leaders and to teachers. As in other countries, many teachers in Sweden cherish their constraints and are finding it difficult to begin to do their own curricular thinking.

Alongside this concern for the revision and reform of the curriculum has been a concern over the development of the comprehensive school. While changes in 'external' organization had taken place, the internal operations of the schools had not changed at the same pace. There were increasing demands for changes in the way schools worked internally. Accordingly, in 1970, a Royal Commission was set up to look into the difficulties being experienced in comprehensive schools, among which were truancy, lack of motivation and apathy among students, and the difficulties of adapting teaching methods to the varying needs and aptitudes of pupils. The Royal Commission on the School's Inner Working (known as SIA) published its report in 1975 and in 1976 Parliament approved a series of reforms which are only gradually being brought about.

As in the developments relating to the curriculum, it will be clear that the SIA reforms also show a significant trend towards decentralization whereby schools would become more autonomous and furthermore would become responsible for making significant changes in their own organization, their curriculum and their working methods. It was recognized that these trends had very important implications for school leaders, who were being called upon to perform roles very different from those which they had performed in the past. The school leader was no longer to be simply an interpreter of central decisions at a local level but was to be much more of a change agent and a co-ordinator of local decisions and development. He or she would be expected to create possibilities for local schools to develop unique solutions to their own unique problems. Accordingly the reforms proposed that all school leaders should undergo compulsory and specialized training in management. These proposals were the origin of the present training programme and in the Government Bill of 1976 three principal aims of the school leader training programme are stated:

(a) The training of school leaders is an element in realizing the goals of the school. The training should therefore be devised in such a way that the school leader, together with staff and students, finds lines of action for the development of the school.

(b) The training should create the opportunity for school leaders to develop the function of administration in collaboration with the staff of the school.

(c) Through the training, the participant should be given the possibility of deepened self-knowledge. Scope should be created for the personal development of the individual participant through interaction with his own staff, his fellow participants and with the training team.

It will be noted that from the outset the notions of change and development are important elements in the fundamental philosophy behind the training programme for school leaders in Sweden and these have not changed. Recent statements by those directing the programme bear this out. Eskil Stegö in his paper to the Gatwick conference (1982) expressed the conviction that the school leader was 'a change agent or at least a facilitator of change' and in the same paper he stated:

The training programme of all Swedish school leaders is seen as a cornerstone of the decentralization process within the school system and also in the renewal of Swedish comprehensive schools. Change and development are key words in the training.

Mats Ekholm (1981) expressed the aims of the scheme thus at the Donaueschingen seminar:

Participants are to be used as a tool to bring about changes through further development of local schools; moreover, the school leader's field of duties, that is to say his role and function are to be extended, and participation in the training programme probably means further development of the school leader's own personality.

It is important to note the sequence and the priorities implicit in these statements. The change and development of schools is the primary aim of the training. There are other aims which involve the development of the school leader's role and the development of his or her personality; but development of the school and improvement of the school are of paramount importance.

The development of school leader training in Sweden

There were other influences on the growth of school management training in Sweden and these should be mentioned. During the 50s and 60s discussions had taken place about a programme of training for school leaders. The school leaders' union and the National Board of Education offered short courses of one week and then of three weeks over a period of some ten years. In the early 1970s the National Board of Education appointed a working party to design a plan for the training of the heads and deputy heads of comprehensive and of upper secondary schools. This was known as the PLUS Commission and its influence on the eventual form which the training programme was to take proved to be considerable. This commission was active for almost two years and had about 85 members. From its deliberations emerged a number of recommendations as to how the training of school leaders was to be carried out. One important area of 'lively debate' reported by Ekholm (1979) concerned how the interaction between theory and practice should be organized within the training programme. Some members favoured the inclusion of simulation exercises as an important feature of the training programme. Others maintained that the point of departure should be the 'concrete and immediate experiences and problems that each participant brought from his own everyday situation. It should be possible to use reality itself as learning material in the training'. (p.22).

Both approaches had been tried out during experimental training which took place prior to and during the work of the PLUS commission. Eventually, the second of these views prevailed. The commission took the view that since the role of the school leader is so dependent on the values and expectations of his colleagues there can be no hope of lasting change in a person's behaviour as a leader without the co-operation of those colleagues. Thus an important principle was established of placing a large proportion of the training programme at each school leader's own school. This has meant that the training as it has evolved has been strongly influenced by the approach of organizational development as compared with the approach which concentrates on developing individual leaders such as we have seen happening in France.

At the same time that the PLUS commission was carrying out this valuable work, the SIA Commission was including in its recommendations proposals for the training of all school leaders and no doubt there was some interplay of ideas between the two commissions. In the event, when the Government Bill was passed in 1976 it proposed that the training to be provided by the National Board of Education for school leaders should be arranged largely according to the recommendations of the PLUS commission. The SIA commission saw the programme of training school leaders as one important means of implementing reforms in schools by emphasizing the roles of school leaders in stimulating local developments in schools. These developments would be initiated by forces within the school and these forces would be given external support. The programme of training was to provide that support.

It will be clear that important decisions were taken at the outset concerning the aims, the organization and the working methods of the programme which have distinguished the Swedish initiative in school leader training from those which have taken place in any other European country. Emphasis has been placed on the head as a change agent and on organizational development as the process whereby changes are to be brought about in schools. It was recognized that change and development in any organization take time and in fact the present programme extends over two years. The ambition during these two years is to make it possible for the development process to start. The PLUS commission had high ambitions, hoping that the development would have progressed further than the stage of initiation and would have become well established but Ekholm now reports (1979) that

the optimism has been somewhat damped since the training

has started on a regular basis. Training today is based on the idea that significant development of schools takes a good deal of time—and seems to require a period of five to seven years. A changing process which has allowed that length of time may have a realistic chance of having tangible effects. (p.9).

Further, he stresses that after the basic period of training, attention has to be paid to the extension of school leader training, to further training of school leaders and to the provision of services to support and sustain developments in schools which have been embarked upon during or on completion of the basic training programme. Instructors will consider that it is important to inculcate a realization that two years of training merely supply a basis for future development. Training equips participants with a readiness which at best can serve as a tool and a prerequisite for advances at their own school. 'Participants leave the programme just as they are on the verge of applying the new methods to as wide a front as possible within their own school'. (Ekholm 1977, p.24).

Having paid a visit to the programme in 1977 and returned for a further visit in 1981 the writer observed a much more guarded optimism evident on the occasion of the second visit among both trainers and trainees about the time necessary to introduce and implement development, particularly given the less favourable climate of the present from the point of view of resources. More school leaders were insisting that the present obstacles to change rendered development more difficult.

The training programme for school leaders in Sweden

In-service education of teachers in Sweden is centred in six regions and based in the towns or cities where there are the six largest teacher training colleges. The National Board of Education is responsible for the school leader training programme and for its budget. The directorate of the programme is based in the in-service training department at Linköping, and is a small unit comprising two professionals, namely Eskil Stegö, a former head, seconded full-time, and Mats Ekholm, a full-time researcher in education. The steering committee of the project is composed of representatives of the association of local *'kommuns'* (communities), of teachers' unions, of the school inspectors of county boards and of the in-service department at Linköping.

The directorate is responsible for the 'training teams' which are based in eight regions of Sweden. Two teams are further divided into two sub-regions. Each regional team has a full-time co-ordinator who is usually a head on secondment or a county inspector. Other members of the training teams are either heads, county inspectors or educational psychologists who are seconded to work part-time with the team.

While the school leaders of a particular town or village are being trained, the team is supplemented by the appropriate school director for the area, and also by a political representative of the municipality, who is chosen by its council.

The directorate provides training for the co-ordinators of the training teams and also for the members of the teams. The number of days of such training which have been provided are as follows:

School year	Days with all trainers	Days with co-ordinators only
1976/77	12	11
1977/78	11	9
1978/79	7	17
1979/80	6	13
1980/81	7	11
1981/82	16	—

The directorate has also produced a considerable amount of teaching material as well as being responsible for a programme of research and evaluation of the project.

THE PARTICIPANTS IN THE TRAINING PROGRAMME

The programme of training is compulsory for all school leaders from all types of schools, including comprehensive and upper secondary schools. Where possible all school leaders in a particular *'kommun'* participate simultaneously in the same training programme. This means the heads and their deputies participate in the same training programme. From the inception of the programme in 1976 until 1980 about 600 school leaders were trained annually and by that year about half the 4,500 school leaders had been trained. It had been intended to complete the training in about ten years but owing to the difficult economic situation there has been some slowing down of the programme and at present about 330 school leaders are being trained each year.

THE COMPONENTS OF THE TRAINING PROGRAMME

The programme extends over two academic years and contains three elements. Firstly, there are 20 course or conference days when all the participants come together at a residential conference centre or hotel. The 'course periods' as they are described are six to eight in number and each course period lasts two to four days. During these 'course periods' participants work on themes which are to form the basis of on-the-job training back in their schools. They study their own school and its working processes and also study their own roles as leaders in those processes. There is some theoretical input and there are practical problem-solving activities. At Windsor, Ekholm reported that this part of the programme had been described as:

> relatively unstructured encounters with reflective talks as a dominating component and during which the trainers review the quality of work achieved. Of course lectures are given, or brief introductions to the areas dealt with but there are also a great number of problem-solving tasks, planning sessions and evaluative discussions. [See Hegarty (Ed), 1983.]

There are about 30 members in a course group and much work is carried out in small groups of five to seven members. The working methods used are based on assumptions about group psychology and as well as the study of professional problems arising from school situations there is also study of the dynamics of the group itself. School leaders with different experience are deliberately mixed together in the groups.

The periods in between the 'course periods' are known as 'home periods' and are considered to be an equally important part of the total programme. School leaders are expected to work on themes related to the training programme during these 'home periods' and are supposed to devote 1/10 of their time to this work. The work begins with observation of the working processes of the school and moves through a situational analysis to the initiation of development in the school. The team of trainers requires participants to formulate their own home assignments and they make various visits to the schools during the 'home periods' to discuss developments. During the 'home periods' the participants also work together with other local participants in study circles.

In addition to the 'course periods' and the 'home periods' there is a third element in the programme. Each participant is expected to undergo a period of practical society-orientated experience in the locality where he or she works. During these periods the school leader works in a commercial concern or in a local department of welfare or social services. This period was originally four weeks but owing to economic difficulties has been reduced to ten days. The purpose of this experience is for school leaders to get to know the conditions in which parents work and which pupils will meet when they leave school. In one study of this experience Eskil Stegö reported that 35 per cent of participants had worked in mechanical engineering work and about 10 per cent had worked in each of the following: the wood processing industry, the iron and mining industries and in farming.

THE FINANCING OF THE TRAINING PROGRAMME
The National Board of Education is responsible for the budget of the programme. The total budget for the period 1978–79 was nine million Swedish crowns. Replacements are found for the school leaders during the 'course periods' and during the period of society-orientated work outside the school. Negotiations between the government and the heads' trade union established how much of a school leader's time in school should be devoted to the programme, namely 1/10 of normal working hours or 40 days. Therefore, substitutes are employed for some 70 days' equivalent per participant during the programme and the cost of this provision of substitutes accounts for 2/3 of the programme's annual budget.

THE CONTENT OF THE TRAINING PROGRAMME
As has already been stated in this study, the main emphasis in the Swedish programme of school leader training is on the development of the school leader's role as a change agent or a facilitator of change, and upon the process whereby change and development may be brought about in a school. The two members of the directorate have documented fully their approach to these issues, notably in the following four reports:

Report No. 1 *School Leader Education in*
Sweden Ekholm, 1977
Report No. 2 *The Role of the School Leader* Stegö, 1978
Report No. 3 *Research in Education — Does*
it Matter? Ekholm, 1979
Report No. 4 *Training School Leaders in*
Sweden Stegö, 1979

Eskil Stegö (1979) explains how the programme takes as a starting point theories and models of organizational change.

If school leaders are to fulfil a role as facilitators of educational change it is essential that they have knowledge of schools as organizations, of the process of change and of their own role as leaders in that process. (p.6).

The training programme recognizes the necessity and the difficulty of bridging the gap between theory and practice; between the training which takes place away from the school and the real life of the school where actual development is to take place. A framework of organizational development is offered to the particpants and they are given the responsibility for applying it to their schools in collaboration with their staffs.

The school leader has the main responsibility for working on the problems, for testing and experimenting and for taking the risks involved in seeking a solution. It is he who must evaluate the solutions and decide whether they are acceptable or not. (Stegö, 1979, p.7).

The school leaders' active participation is based on a

70

systematic 'mapping-out' which leads to a planned programme. Considerable emphasis is laid upon the importance of forward planning and the need for a readiness to modify initial planning in the light of experience and of reality.

Stegö (1979, p.8) has set out the suggested process to be followed in Fig. 1.

This approach is used to help school leaders to work systematically. The strategy adopted is to build a plan in consultation with the school leader, beginning with the observation of reality.

In a report on school leader education (1977), Ekholm outlines his own framework for the developmental process which is built upon his participation in attempted changes within Swedish comprehensive schools. This work suggests that there are four phases which make up the developmental process: preparation, accommodation, application and circulation. In the same report Ekholm describes strategies for starting the developmental process including the method whereby the members of the school, for the benefit of

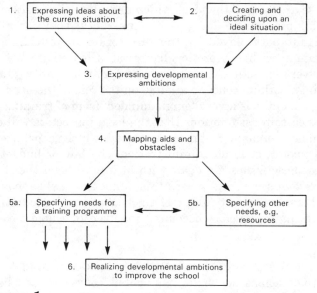

Figure 1

themselves and for each other, together describe the 'daily shape of everyday activities' in the school. These 'descriptions of reality' are then set against the members' preoccupations. During the first stage of the training programme great emphasis is placed on getting the school leaders to describe 'the reality' of their schools. Participants then analyse their observations and determine the long-range and the acute problem areas. They then decide, after consultation with members of the school staff, which of these problems is to receive first priority. Together with their staffs they decide what local developmental work they are to attempt during and following the two-year training period.

A further idea which is prominent in the theoretical underpinning of the training programme is the definition of the change agent as a catalyst and a process-aid (Havelock, 1973). In his paper delivered at Donaueschingen (1981) Ekholm refers to the possible roles which a leader can adopt in the development process. The least practical is, he suggests, the 'solution finder' and 'it can be considerably more effective to act as a catalyst or midwife when improvements to local organization are envisaged'.

These are some of the ideas which underlie the process of the training programme and give it a coherence. They reveal the important part played by the directorate in providing the programme with a theoretical background as well as a positive framework for action, thus injecting a dynamic quality into the training. With its concentration upon the role of the head as a change agent it is a very 'single-minded' form of training and makes certain assumptions that the local inspectors will deal with more mundane and routine matters which school leaders must master, such as administration, the law or budgeting. Where these issues are dealt with at a local level the school leaders feel secure but where this is not so, newly-appointed school leaders in particular feel a need for some basic training in such matters, before becoming involved in school development.

A REGIONAL TRAINING PROGRAMME FOR SCHOOL LEADERS
On two occasions the writer has visited 'course periods' being held in the south-east region of Sweden. The co-ordinator for

this regional training programme is Nils Lagervall, who is head of a comprehensive school in the town of Mjölby and is seconded full-time to the project. He is also a leading member of the School-leaders' Association in Sweden. This study is much indebted to him for his warm hospitality, wise help and guidance, and patient translation.

The course periods both took place at well-appointed hotels which provided comfortable accommodation. The day's programme began at 8.00 a.m., with sessions each lasting for two hours; there were five sessions in a day. Lunch was taken at 11.30 a.m. and the evening meal at 6.30 p.m. Most of the sessions were conducted around a large table in a relaxed, informal seminar style, which encouraged considerable plenary discussion and also work in small groups.

A typical day during the first visit took the theme of 'observation' as this course period was at the beginning of the training programme. The first session was devoted to planning ways in which observation would be carried out in the classrooms of a local school. A framework for observation was devised and then a large part of the rest of the day was spent in visiting local schools in the area to gain experience in making systematic observations. The latter part of the day was devoted to analysing the observations which had been made, and to discussion of the type of systematization which might be of use to a school leader.

When asked to summarize the ways in which his team's strategies had changed over the year, Nils Lagervall said that there had been one major change in the team's strategy. Originally, they had worked within a more rigid structure. Even before the training began they knew in detail what the contents of the 'course periods' would be. Then the content had been a combination of the competences they thought they had in the team; now they tried to respond to what the different course groups thought they needed. This development had resulted in a decrease in quality but, he hoped, in an increase in meaningfulness for the participants.

SOME REACTIONS OF SCHOOL LEADERS ATTENDING THE 'COURSE PERIODS'
Most were very willing to discuss their experiences of the

training programme and many commented favourably.
Typical reactions were as follows.

- The course was unlike any that they had attended
  before.
- The attempt to change attitudes and to generate change
  was necessary but was a very lengthy task.
- Some felt more confident to try out new ideas and to open
  up possibilities.
- The emphasis on work in small groups was much
  appreciated. It developed openness, frankness and self-
  awareness during the course.
- There was scepticism at first, particularly on receiving
  early papers containing psychological and sociological
  jargon. (In response to criticism, two early papers were
  being rewritten at Linköping).
- Case studies had limited value and likewise simulation
  exercises. They lacked reality.
- Some were disturbed by the apparent lack of overall plan
  of the training programme.
- A politician felt that the training was too theoretical and
  should deal with more practical problems.
- The most valuable work was done in their own schools
  during the home periods. The job of the training teams
  was to provide techniques and to catalyse discussion.
- The participation of so many heads in the planning was
  much appreciated.

The evaluation of school leader training in Sweden

The evaluation of the results of in-service education is
notoriously difficult for many reasons, not least of which is the
problem of distinguishing those changes in a person which
may be attributed to the specific training which is being
evaluated from those changes which have been brought about
by other influences. This study has already emphasized the
very many pressures which come to bear onto school leaders
nowadays. These pressures come from many sources, both from
inside and outside the school, and may either encourage or
inhibit change. A programme of school leader training is only

one such influence and it is extremely difficult to evaluate the effectiveness of such training in bringing about changes in the structure, organization, climate or relationships within a school. Nethertheless, the evaluation of the school leader training programme has been actively pursued in Sweden, where there is a tradition of careful analysis and evaluation. The work that has been carried out and is in the process of being carried out remains almost the sole example of substantial evaluation of a school leader training programme which has been undertaken in Western Europe.

The results of the evaluation programmes relating to the school leader training programme were reported on by Eskil Stegö at the Gatwick Conference and by Mats Ekholm at the Windsor Workshop. More detailed reference to both these reports will be made in the later chapter of this study which is concerned with evaluation. The reports also contain a number of significant conclusions which have been reached by the directorate and by others about the school leader training programme in Sweden which has been in progress for seven years. These may serve as an appropriate conclusion to this case study.

SOME CONCLUSIONS ABOUT THE SCHOOL LEADER TRAINING IN SWEDEN

The general conclusion from several evaluations of the training programme in Sweden is that to date the training is welcomed. The reactions to the training which were reported to this writer by school leaders were certainly very positive. The scheme is running to capacity and in spite of some slowing down of the programme owing to economic difficulties, the original thrust is being maintained and will result in the training of all school leaders in the foreseeable future, even if a little later than was originally intended. This will be a remarkable achievement. Nevertheless, the members of the directorate are very self-critical, and make the following points about the programme so far.

One of the problems arises from the aim of providing a training for individual school leaders to bring about developments in individual schools. The directorate report difficulty in meeting individual requirements during course periods. They go so far as to say that the individualizing of requirements during lecture periods 'seldom happens' and is 'exceptional' when it does.

Several difficulties are reported concerning the 'home periods', the first of which concerns the way in which the trainers and the participants agree what should be done during these. A lack of clarity about the role of trainers in relation to the participants weakens the contract between trainer and participant to undertake a particular piece of work during the 'home periods'. There is also evidence to show that some participants are doing their 'home work' not because they really want to change their school, nor even to understand it better, but in order to have something to show to other participants and to the trainers when they attend the next course period. However, the proportion of school leaders who work in this way is thought to be small, mainly because trainers usually accept the participants' own choice of developmental tasks. A further source of difficulty concerning home periods is that it has not been possible to carry out satisfactory checks on the extent to which school leaders take advantage of and respect the various agreements regarding the time which is to be devoted to the training programme during the 'home periods'. The agreement for budgeting to provide substitute teaching staff in order to give the school leader time for this work is to allow ten per cent of working time in school for this purpose. This amounts to some 40 days during the two-year programme, or to about four hours per week. However, the average amount of time. claimed by participants as being spent on the work is only about 2.16 hours per week and the amounts of time spent on these activities in the eight training areas in Sweden vary between an average of 2.4 hours and 1.8 hours. As these claims are based on self-declarations they probably represent over-estimates.

Some fundamental concerns are reported by the directorate about methodology and in particular they stress that trainers have not yet fully understood or explained why and how adults learn. The average age of school leaders is fairly advanced —approximately 50 years. To quote Mats Ekholm (1981): 'Empirical knowledge regarding the developmental psychology of persons aged between 40 and 50 is not very impressive'. Nevertheless, trainers have to proceed on certain assumptions about how adults learn and consequently the training in this field is to a great extent based upon supposition and obviously entails certain unavoidable risks. One such supposition or belief is that learning takes place more effectively in 'actual situations'. Participants are encouraged to grasp the chance to learn from significant situations when they arise in school, as such experience can be much more effective than learning from documents, from simulation games or from models which have been designed for training purposes. However, for such learning to take place, participants must be prepared to use the natural situations of daily reality and not all have this preparedness. Whether one learns more effectively at 50 in planned or unplanned situations remains an important question.

Likewise, as in other countries, the relationship between theory and practice remains a thorny problem in the Swedish training programmes. While every effort is made to integrate theory with practice by combining them in action during the training and demonstrating to participants that theory and practice must be one, the directorate report that obvious weakness can still be perceived in this respect.

The evolving role of the trainer has already been referred to and Mats Ekholm expresses his concern particularly over the readiness of trainers to participate in group discussions and indeed to play a positive role in those discussions as 'a sort of inquisitorial catalyst':

> It is often important that someone accepts the responsibility of being a sort of 'teasel' in the discussions between participants, to help them to get more out of their discussions both as regards the subject matter of the discussion and as regards the group dynamics. (1977, p. 29).

Current trends and the future of the training programme in Sweden

During a discussion with Mats Ekholm, the writer sought information about changes in emphasis in the programme during the period from 1976 to 1981 and the co-director of the project made the following points:

1. Originally, there was considerable emphasis on relationships, on sensitivity training and on group dynamics. While this remains an important element in the training, there has been a shift of emphasis towards the development of the leadership role and to the development of the organization. This meant more interest in personal development, in group development and in educational development. Staff development has assumed greater importance: how to delegate, motivate and involve other staff. The trainers have to make more significant inputs in the fields of:
   (a) organization theory, and
   (b) organizational development.
2. Increased emphasis was now being given to the 'home periods'. How to make the most use of 'home periods' had always been a problem. Pressures of work had always reduced the amount of time actually devoted to the training programme by participants. However, there was now more detailed preparation for the 'home periods' and more planning sessions were now built into the 'course periods'.
3. Associated with the problem of how to make the most effective use of 'home periods' was the problem of visits to the schools by members of the training team. The current aim was a frequency of about four visits over the two-year period. This was probably not enough. The role of the trainer as visitor or consultant was still being developed. There were some advantages in two people visiting at the same time, to gain two perspectives of the school situation.

What developments would Mats Ekholm like to see in the future of the programme? Firstly, he hoped that the programme would not suffer any further financial cuts. (The annual intake had been halved from 600 to 300). There was already an informal shift of emphasis whereby such elements as budgeting, administration and law had been removed from the national programme to be dealt with at local level. This trend was leading to the notion of a three-year course, the first year dealing with the administrative aspects of the school leader's job and the second two years dealing with the developmental aspects of the job. The next stage that he would like to see considered was an extension of the course forward for a further two years to take account of developments in the schools, and to ensure that such developments took place. He estimated that it took one and a half years to initiate movement in the school leadership and a further one and a half years for that movement to begin to reach class-teacher level. Full acceptance of change in a school could take from five to seven years.

Some conclusions

The programme for training school leaders in Sweden is very impressive. It is the most ambitious programme in Western Europe and is one from which other countries have much to learn, not least because of the readiness of the co-directors and of the trainers to share their experiences, problems and difficulties with colleagues in other countries. The programme is unique in being a nationally funded programme, which is compulsory for all school leaders and which has clearly stated its aims not only to develop school leaders but also to enable school leaders to develop schools. During a period of economic, social and political change when school leaders face such an uncertain future, a programme which focuses upon the school leader as a change agent warrants serious attention. Such a programme as has been developed in Sweden is also very costly, but that fact poses a serious challenge to all member states in that it raises the question of what investment we are prepared to make in the future of our schools and of our children.

Whatever may be said of the ideological aims of the programme which are concerned with organizational development, the Swedes are also evolving a methodology of training which deserves serious consideration. By placing a substantial element of the training in the schools themselves, by using real situations as teaching material, by involving the rest of the staff as well as the school leader and by exploring the possibilities of the trainer as consultant, they are creating a further dimension of in-service training.

England

The second example of a programme designed to provide training for individual heads and deputy heads of secondary schools is taken from England. The previous example, drawn from France, was of courses initiated from a national centre, whereas the English example is of a programme provided by a regional centre, specifically established for the purpose and known as the North West Educational Management Centre. In contrast to the development of regional centres in France and Sweden which we have seen to have their origins in national initiatives taken centrally, the NWEMC, as it is referred to, originated in a regional initiative taken by a number of local education authorities acting together as a consortium as long ago as 1972.

However, before examining the work of NWEMC in more detail, it is necessary to set it into the context of educational developments in England and Wales. It is to be noted that Scotland is not included in this account and, in fact, possesses its own centre for the training of the heads and senior staff of secondary schools, known as the Scottish Centre for Studies in School Administration. An account of the work of this Centre was given to the Gatwick Conference of 1982 and to the Council of Europe course at Kristiansand in the same year.

The system of education in England and Wales differs from those of their European neighbours by being highly decentralized. While it is true to say that the Department of Education and Science has since 1977 begun to play a more interventionist role, particularly in influencing the development of the school curriculum, nevertheless the Local Education Authorities (LEAS), of which there are 104, continue to exercise a traditional independence and autonomy. In fact, it is only recently that the government has taken an initiative to promote and co-ordinate the training of senior staff in schools and then only following mounting pressure from the profession. However, prior to this initiative taken in 1983 a variety of training programmes had already developed, in a somewhat haphazard way and in an uneven fashion, throughout the country. There were many providers of these diverse programmes including the local authorities themselves, universities, polytechnics, the Open University and many other institutions, usually acting quite independently.

In sketching in the background to the development of this rich diversity of provision or this somewhat chaotic situation, depending upon which way it is regarded, a further factor needs to be borne in mind and that is the relative independence of the head in England and Wales and the historical significance of the 'headmaster tradition'. While many heads would say that their legendary power is being progressively eroded by the increased influence of the unions, parents, financial constraints, the increasing intervention of the Department of Education and Science (DES) and growing demands for accountability, nevertheless their degree of independence and autonomy remains considerable. Pautler, an external observer, commented in her paper to the EEC seminar at Pont-à-Mousson (1982), 'It is beyond doubt that in the English system the power of decision of the head remains considerable and he is not so conscious as his European colleagues of the weight of a hierarchy'.

Baron in a paper published in 1956 traced the development in the mid-nineteenth century of the distinctive 'headmaster tradition' in the English public schools and showed how the tradition was later emulated with minor modification in the new maintained secondary schools of the early twentieth century. A powerful and distinctive role concept emerged, of the benevolent autocrat, feared and loved by staff and pupils, a leader of undisputed authority but also very much a teacher, particularly of senior pupils, who adopted a paternalistic, pastoral relationship to assistant staff as well as to pupils. Baron noted few signs of significant change at the time of writing.

Meredydd Hughes in his paper to the Windsor workshop gives a scholarly account of the progress made in England and Wales towards achieving a new understanding of the role and tasks of the head. Some reference has already been made to Hughes' distinguished work in this field and he has recently

(1981) been responsible for a research project supported by the DES which surveyed, and was entitled, 'The Professional Development Provision for Senior Staff in Schools and Colleges' and which added weight to the increasing demands for a national initiative.

Hughes quotes the work of Bernbaum (1973, 1976) as illustrating how slowly the tradition changed. Contemporary secondary heads, whether of grammar schools or of comprehensive schools, still saw the role and tasks in traditional terms, with a strong emphasis on 'pastoral care' as it became known in England, and on the human relationships aspect of the job. Bates (1970) found that while some activities were dropped or shared with other levels of staff as schools increased in size, heads in his sample of 50 comprehensive schools showed a perceptible reluctance to break with the main sources of direct contact with pupils. Benn and Simon (1970) expressed anxiety concerning the adverse effect on the heads of large comprehensive schools of seeking to adhere to the 'headmaster tradition': 'All too many of these heads are carrying far too big a burden of their school's success on their shoulders, because of their desire to live up to traditional ideals of being a "good headmaster".' In the view of this writer this dedication to a special vocation persists among many of the heads he has encountered and to some extent accounts for the reluctance of some heads to see themselves either as administrators or managers or to seek training which may have an administrative or managerial emphasis originating outside the educational world, in the fields of industry or commerce.

However, during the 1970s some practising heads were beginning to advocate a more managerial approach to their role. Furthermore, the growth of large comprehensive schools led to more elaborate hierarchial structures and salary differentials which meant that differentiation of the head's functions became necessary. A large comprehensive school could have as many as three deputy heads, a larger number of heads of academic subjects and a substantial number of 'pastoral' posts, as they became known. The latter required teachers to be responsible for subdivisions of the school's population such as years or 'houses' (vertical sub-divisions of the school having their origin in the public boarding schools). The secondary schools thus became more bureaucratic in management and there was a growing concern for delegation, for clarifying objectives and for establishing structures for decision-making. King (1968) analysed the head's role as the 'chief executive' but accepted that there were also traditional (or ritualistic) and charismatic elements which illustrated the persistence of the 'headmaster tradition'.

Hughes' own work in developing the proposition that the head is simultaneously the 'leading professional' and the 'chief executive' has already been referred to in this study and some of his findings given (1972, 1973, 1975, 1977). Again, two independent factors were revealed by the empirical evidence: a traditional factor which could be identified with the 'head-master tradition' and an innovating factor concerned with bringing about educational change. The evidence also showed that in relation to the chief executive aspect of the role, there was a significant tendency for heads who considered that they were granted a high degree of autonomy by external authority to act positively in their internal administration, taking initiatives and delegating effectively to members of staff. The converse also applied (Hughes 1978).

More recently practising heads have emphasized the increased pressures of the job and the need for 'survival skills'. Nockels (1981) investigating the problems of the newly-appointed head in his or her first year provides evidence from interviews that essential information considered necessary for survival was not readily available and that problems arising in the establishment of good human relationships, particularly with staff, were paramount. Other issues which were beginning to loom large were the management of a contracting institution, the growth of pressure groups and the school's public relations. This concern for the importance of external relations had been noted by Glatter (1980) and was to figure prominently in the analysis of head's tasks which was developed by Morgan and Hall (1982). This analysis is given in full earlier in this study and represents a contemporary view of what heads of secondary schools in England and Wales have to do. A further valuable contribution to this field is a three-year research project carried out by the National Federation for Educational Research, 'The first years of headship in the secondary school' which began in 1982. The aim will be to discover the demands made on new heads and the strategies used by them during their first years in office. This study will involve some 250 heads who have been in post for three to eight years.

Some reference, however brief, must also be made to the role of the deputy head in the English secondary school because, as has been indicated already, there may be two or three such appointments in a comprehensive school and the role has assumed considerable importance in the field of school management as well as providing the major training ground for headship. A study of deputy headship in 233 northern secondary schools was carried out by Burnham (1964, 1968). He tested out the hypothesis that deputy heads would be vulnerable to role conflict by virtue of their intermediate positions in five areas: school organization, concern for teachers, teaching, relation to children, relation to society. He found that the pattern of such conflict was not uniform and there was considerable role ambiguity because the deputy's role was essentially anomalous and ill-defined. Williams (1979), in a study of 38 deputies in 28 north London comprehensive schools, found that there was specialization among deputies, particularly between male and female deputies:

> Increased specialization tends to cast deputies in stereotyped roles: male deputies in the 'demanding' role of curriculum planning or timetabling and female deputies in the 'caring' role of pastoral care and girls' welfare'. (p.44).

Todd and Dennison (1978), reporting on a study of 11 comprehensive schools in the north of England, found that not all the schools had specialized roles for their deputies; the schools could be placed along a continuum from shared responsibilities in all tasks to a clear division of roles, curriculum, pastoral care and administration being usually identified as separate tasks. Deputies all saw themselves as members, together with the head, of the school's management team. Such management teams have become a common feature of secondary schools in England and Wales in the late 70s and 80s and may include as many as seven members of staff since the post of 'senior teacher' became recognized for salary purposes in addition to the post of deputy head. There are some indications however that the size of management teams may be progressively reduced as the number on school rolls falls and staffing is reduced accordingly. It is the writer's experience from encounters with many deputy heads that while in many cases nowadays their roles may be more clearly defined, there remain many who accumulate a wide variety of 'odd jobs' which are not performed by anybody else. Consequently, the role of deputy head may lack coherence, and often amounts to day-to-day crisis management.

The training of heads and of senior staff in England

Before presenting a case study of a training programme in one particular regional centre, an attempt must be made to summarize the situation regarding professional development provision in England and Wales. This is a very difficult task and will be dealt with most inadequately because of the very wide diversity of provision, the very large number of providers, the exceptional degree of local and regional independence and the lack of any real co-ordination. However, the report of the DES sponsored research project, 'Professional Development Provision in Schools and Colleges' (Hughes et al., 1981) provides very useful documented evidence of what is happening.

There is now no doubt as to the expressed need for training which was articulated by all the teachers' unions to Hughes and his team. They point to a very uneven provision of management training between one region and another and between one local authority and another. The Secondary Heads' Association referred to the 'uneven and unstable patchwork of current provision in different parts of the country' and also commented on the very uneven quality of what is being provided. This association has mounted a sustained campaign for the establishment of a national Staff College, which would promote good practice in leadership and management and be at the centre of a network of regionally accessible centres for in-service education for leadership at various levels. The

National Association of Headteachers had long advocated the provision of management courses for heads and deputy heads and had some experience of providing annual residential courses for its members. A major source of grievance and resentment reported to Hughes and his team was the very wide difference in the financial support provided by local education authorities for participants attending courses. Hughes describes these differences as 'unacceptably great'. Some impression of the size of the problem and of the diversity of the present provision may be derived from the Hughes report. In the 104 local education authorities there are some 4,500 secondary schools. There was by 1980 a substantial provision of long award-bearing courses specializing in education management, or containing a significant component of education management. 86 courses were provided by 24 universities, 13 polytechnics and 21 other colleges of higher education. In 1980 some 1,600 students qualified, 80 per cent of them by part-time study. This number excludes the many undertaking part-time study via the Open University 'distance learning' courses, which are establishing a considerable reputation both in the UK and abroad. In the same year 100 people were studying for higher degrees in educational management. Most of the students involved in these long award-bearing courses are aspiring heads and deputies seeking to improve their qualifications in a climate increasingly unfavourable for promotion, but there are also some primary and secondary heads following such courses. 20 per cent of those attending such courses at the Sheffield Polytechnic were already in posts as heads. There are obvious problems for practising heads in being absent from their schools to follow long full-time courses. However, Hughes reports that these courses show a steady and consistent growth and that practitioners' scepticism has vanished.

In the area of short non-award-bearing courses he reports that provision is 'patchy and uneven'. The best is very good but in many areas provision is fortuitous and unplanned. There is great variety and some confusion in what is being provided and a well-resourced national initiative is desirable. Most such courses are of two to five days' duration and many are spread over several weeks or even months. Local education authorities provided some two thirds of all short courses in

1980 and there were 696 such courses. Over 20,000 short course registrations were recorded, although there may have been some duplication of numbers. Four LEAs provided 170 of the courses and an average provision was ten courses. 46 LEAs reported three or fewer courses of professional development for senior staff in secondary schools. This irregular pattern had developed over a decade with the minimum of co-ordination or conscious planning. The fact that most of the development had been at LEA and at institutional level meant that no one person had a clear appreciation of the kind or distribution of the provision available. The Hughes report (1981) recommended that to meet this situation a national initiative was needed to improve the provision not by imposing a national scheme but by co-ordinating, supporting and encouraging local initiatives. He proposed the creation of a School Management Unit which would be independent of the DES, would act as a catalyst and a resource, would undertake research and development and would maintain links with other countries. Meanwhile, the DES was giving careful consideration to the matter and was examining ways in which the initiative might be taken. It was important that the initiative should not fail by being conceived in unimaginative and inadequate terms or by creating inappropriate structures. This might lead to a loss of momentum and a dissipation of goodwill among the many agencies already very active in the field. The English genius for what one member of Her Majesty's Inspectorate called 'retrospective planning' was being called for.

In organizational terms the major problem centred not so much on the activities of the national unit, if there was to be one, but upon what the appropriate local organization was to be and where actual training was to be carried out. While some large local authorities sustained well-developed programmes of in-service training others clearly did not possess the resources to maintain continuous training programmes for senior staff. The Hughes report commented favourably on a number of instances in which LEAs were co-operating with each other and with institutions of higher education, as a means of improving the training opportunities for heads and other senior staff. His team considered that such regional initiatives 'were indicative of a pattern which shows promise of being capable of further development'. Of the examples given the report stated:

> The North West Educational Management Centre, established in 1972 as a consortium of all the LEAs in the north west of England (18 in number), is the most noteworthy example of continuing LEA collaboration in this area. (p.206).

The Director of NWEMC had expressed the view to the research team that it was the LEAs who controlled the Centre and it was they who were:

> in the best position to identify their training needs and who had a common interest in and a responsibility for maintaining the quality of headship, the efficiency of school management and the most effective use of resources. (p.206).

A structure had been developed over the years which enabled courses to be organized so as to respond to the perceived needs of course participants and of their employing authorities. The report concluded that this was a considerable achievement and that it was not surprising that the venture had attracted widespread interest. NWEMC was selected by Hughes as one of the case studies which featured in his report and also in the paper which he presented to the Windsor workshop. This centre has also had some influence over the development of other regional activities in England and notably served as a model for the development of a training initiative in Northern Ireland, which began in 1980.

The national initiative from the Department of Education and Science took place in December 1982 when three projects were announced with the aim: 'to develop the expertise needed to organize schools and their curriculum, and to handle resources'. When the initiative was announced, the Education Secretary, Sir Keith Joseph, stated:

> The standards of our schools—academic, moral and cultural—are set by the heads and the senior staff within them. It is essential that they should be fully equipped for

the difficult tasks that face them, including those tasks created by falling school rolls. At the moment there is insufficient management training for headteachers and we, together with the LEAs, want to increase it.

The three elements of the initiative were:

1. The creation of a National Development Centre which would provide a national focus for management training for schools. The Centre would evaluate existing courses, develop new materials, set up a resource bank and disseminate such materials, foster the establishment of new regional schemes for providing basic and other courses and develop links with regional committees for in-service training.
2. The release of experienced heads and senior staff for one term secondments. These would provide opportunities for visits to schools and other institutions, seminars, private study, encounters with managers from other fields of education, commerce and industry. It was expected that those who have completed one term training opportunities would in turn contribute to the staffing and organizing of basic courses.
3. The development of basic short courses in school management which would be 'a regional response to regional needs'. These courses were to be of an aggregated minimum of 20 full days' duration. While in most regions such courses existed the Education Secretary stressed that 'many local education authorities and institutions offer management courses which, though admirable in themselves, do not match the requirements of the new scheme'. Approval of such courses would need to be sought from Her Majesty's Inspectors responsible for regions.

The National Development Centre was located in the School of Education of the University of Bristol and 27 institutions have been identified which are able to offer one-term training opportunities. The new scheme came into operation in the summer of 1983.

The North West Educational Management Centre

The Centre was founded in September 1972 and was able to draw on the experience of a DES sponsored three-year action research programme to train secondary heads in the principles and skills of management and organization, which had been based in the University of Manchester. Schools were increasing in size and complexity as comprehensive reorganization took place, and were confronted with formidable pressures from many directions. Many heads were becoming aware that they would benefit from some specific training for the performance of their roles. At the conclusion of the research project, which had been directed by a recently retired member of Her Majesty's Inspectorate who had been responsible for the North West region of England, the local education authorities (there are now 18) decided with DES approval to set up an Educational Management Centre in the then Padgate College of Education (later to become the North Cheshire College). The close links between the Centre and both the LEAs and the DES through its Inspectorate provided an independence which was a unique feature during the early years of its existence. A group of experienced heads had advised the University on the original scope, pattern and content of courses and this undoubtedly influenced the development of the Centre's philosophy which was to approach the management of schools not from an academic or theoretical standpoint alone, but to ensure that the courses were rooted and grounded in the contemporary practice and experience of secondary schools. Furthermore, on the recommendation of the original working party, the title of 'study-conferences' was adopted to emphasize the importance which was attached to participation and the extent to which participants were expected to regard themselves as partners in their own learning. LEAs nominate members and in the majority of cases are responsible for the full costs of their attendance. They are also encouraged to nominate occasionally administrators, advisers or inspectors as well as heads and deputy heads. Great benefit has been gained from the fact that members come from a wide spectrum of LEAs in a large geographical region thus ensuring a wide background of varying experience. The numbers on each study-conference are limited to about 30 to ensure group sizes of seven or eight. Experience has shown that there is an optimum size for study groups if the quality of discussion and the degree of individual involvement are to be maintained.

After very careful consideration of the impact on individual members and upon their schools of heads being absent, it was felt to be unreasonable to upset the normal working of schools for longer than one term. Accordingly, a pattern of attendance was established which was equivalent in length to one month's full-time study. This consisted of one residential week at the beginning and at the end of the course, interspersed with six one-day sessions usually at weekly intervals extending over one term. With minor modifications this pattern has persisted and while some concern has been expressed by members about the difficulties of attending for single days, some benefits have been gained by members arriving with their school problems in the forefront of their minds.

The permanent full-time staff of the Centre is small and consists of a Director, a Deputy Director and an Assistant Director (Primary), all of whom have direct experience of headship. In addition there is an Administrative Assistant and clerical support. An important feature of the staffing policy has been the development of a body of consultant tutors who are all practising heads. These consultant tutors take part in the planning and assessment of courses as well as acting as discussion group leaders. They have been an invaluable support for the Centre staff, helping them to keep in touch with schools, identifying training needs, subjecting teaching to critical scrutiny and devising new teaching resources. They have also provided the opportunity for professional exchange and discussion which has been an immense source of strength enabling the basic philosophy of the Centre to be continuously re-examined, in the light of contemporary conditions in schools.

The aims of the study-conferences are to develop individuals in the following ways:

To press members to re-examine and to re-appraise their own ideas, convictions, attitudes, prejudices and practices, and to encourage members to develop a distinct philosophy of their own and to build up a code of practice, developing techniques and skills, through which this philosophy can be expressed in action.

The directing staff aim to instil confidence in conference members both personally and professionally. This aim is facilitated by providing the opportunity to meet professional colleagues in a relaxed atmosphere away from the stresses and strains of their daily life, to share problems and to gain mutual support from each other. Pre-course visits are made by the directing staff to all nominated members in order to provide reassurance and to identify the special interests, experience and skills of course members as well as to identify particular problems and anxieties.

Whilst the exact content of each study-conference may vary, a basic pattern has emerged in which high quality lectures and teaching material are considered to be intrinsic elements. Key lectures, introducing the basic themes of the teaching programme, are supported by

(a) subsequent discussion in plenary session, and
(b) the presentation and examination in depth of teaching material, which is designed to illustrate the philosophical and practical implications of the topic in question.

Group discussion constitutes a major part of every teaching programme and the teaching materials put before·members are based either upon case studies or simulations which originate in first-hand experience of schools in the north west of England, or increasingly, exercises have been devised making use of material which members bring from their own schools, thus adding a further element of realism to the discussions which follow. A short reading list is given to each member before the conference and a fuller bibliography is available. However, while members are encouraged to read professional books while at the Centre this has always proved to be a problem area and many do not find time for this activity.

A typical programme for a study-conference includes, in the

first residential week, a study of contemporary schools and society, an examination of the school curriculum and its reappraisal and a substantial practical exercise in planning the contraction of a school faced with a falling roll. Single-day sessions include techniques and skills involved in timetabling, staff selection, and evaluation together with the study of topics such as school organization, decision-making and staff development. The final residential week includes sessions on the law, interpersonal relationships and a second major exercise in planning for the future. The programme has undergone a considerable process of change and evolution over the years and more recently topics such as the curriculum, the multi-cultural society, stress in schools and the need for long-term future planning have assumed great importance in the programme design. The concern for interpersonal relationships remains a major preoccupation and proves to be notoriously difficult to teach. However, it has always been a feature of the 'hidden curriculum' of the Centre. Every effort has been made to cater for the comfort of the members, to maintain high standards of catering and to create a warm social atmosphere. Members of the directorate do not desert the conference but remain in attendance during the evenings of residential sessions. The Centre has even developed its own 'folk rituals' by which it is known in the region. All these seemingly small details contribute to developing the ethos and spirit of a particular conference, as well as building the reputation of a Centre in which participants can have confidence.

In informal conversations with the research fellows who visited the Centre when preparing the Hughes report (1981), many participants indicated that the opportunity for discussion both planned and incidental was a particularly valuable aspect of the conference. The general view was summed up by one member who observed, 'We have learned that there are things which can profitably be discussed with colleagues'. Other comments made to the researchers were as follows:

It has provided me with a range of strategies for areas of my school which I currently recognize as unsatisfactory, i.e.

staff development/assessment, appointments. (*Deputy Head of two years*).

It has helped me to analyse, reflect, improve efficiency and learn from practice and thinking elsewhere. (*Headteacher of fourteen years*).

It has helped to illustrate the diversity of the practice of running schools and made one realize that there are many ways to do the same job, all of which are right. The course stimulated self-knowledge and built confidence. (*Headteacher of two years*).

Many course members paid tribute to the atmosphere created by the directors in caring for the group and developing a sense of commitment. Reference was made to 'each person being cared for as an individual', to the confidence being developed and the feeling was summed up by one member that 'We came away with an experience, not just a body of knowledge'.

The difficulties encountered by the directorate are typical of those providing short in-service training programmes. In composing a programme for such a short period it is more difficult to decide what to leave out than what to include and one is constantly aware of the problem of treating major problems superficially and in insufficient depth. Very little is known about the motivation of heads or senior teachers in a learning situation, or about the teaching methods which are most likely to be accepted or effective. Experience at the Centre shows that some will resent the very idea of being invited to attend a course or conference at all, regarding it as a slur on their already proven competence in a position of responsibility. Some will be doing their best to cloak a feeling of insecurity because they are uncertain about the reasons for their selection. Yet others feel uncomfortable, either through fear of criticism or of inadequacy in defending their particular convictions or practices in open debate. Others, again, resist exposure to any situation in which their prejudices may be challenged. All of them—even those mature and confident enough to recognize that they still have much to learn—will share a feeling of uncertainty at facing a period of in-service training which may be unfamiliar and even threatening. Moreover, they all hide a semi-conscious anxiety lest, to some extent, they will be subject to undercover assessment. For all these confused and conflicting reasons, if their period of training is to be profitable, a major step must be to win their confidence. All that is said by way of introduction and welcome during the pre-course visit and at the opening of the study-conference must create a favourable atmosphere. Initial group discussion must encourage, by subtle and skilful leadership, their willing participation. Topics must be initially eminently practical and of manifest relevance to their schools. Subsequent lectures must be of the highest quality, intellectually stimulating and providing professional challenge. All administrative arrangements and domestic details must be meticulously cared for. All teaching materials, be they documentation or video-taped material must be of high professional quality. A management centre cannot afford to risk the ignominy of being seen as unable to manage. Its credibility will depend precariously on its capacity to maintain the highest professional standards at all times.

A further lesson which has been learned over the years is the extent to which it is important to involve the members in active learning. A number of complex exercises have been devised, some in the form of simulations, others involving 'live' candidates in interviewing situations, under the 'eye' of TV cameras, in which the course members become deeply involved and to which they are prepared to devote considerable time and energy, often culminating in very detailed and professional presentations to their colleagues. Such exercises need to be prepared with the utmost care and attention to detail and be constantly revised to keep them up to date. The extent to which members will be prepared to involve themselves once their interest is engaged is itself a problem because they will often be tired by trying to manage their schools and fulfil course requirements; nevertheless, a rigorous regime has been found to be effective rather than a programme with long spells of free time.

Evaluation of such non-award-bearing courses is also a particular problem. In common with most short course providers, NWEMC provides its members with questionnaires to complete. These questionnaires are detailed and searching, requesting an individual assessment of every aspect of the conference, together with appreciation of its effect upon them-selves, their attitudes and management practice. Such questionnaires are not only helpful to the Centre but also to the participants, who are thus able to assess their personal con-tribution to the learning experience. However, in practice, the questionnaire returns vary greatly in the extent and quality of the analysis and they are not by any means a solution to the problem of course evaluation. Such feedback as has been gained through contract with the LEAs which sponsor members for the study-conferences at NWEMC suggests that the most positive benefits lie in the areas of awareness and increased confidence, combined with a readiness to try out new techniques and skills. However, fundamental changes in attitudes and in philosophy or in the quality of relationships are much slower to mature. Changes in schools are even more difficult to assess. Nevertheless, the LEAs of the North West of England have continued to nominate members for the study-conferences over a period of more than ten years and the Chief Education Officers and Directors of Education who have served on the Steering Committee have given it the imprimatur of their practical support and encouragement.

The Centre has carried out a number of initiatives in recent years. Courses for primary heads have been established since 1977 and work has been undertaken in the field of primary/ secondary continuity. Following the development of links by the writer with the Swedish training programme when he was working at the Centre, two exercises involving organizational developments in schools have taken place in which the role of the consultant in helping to bring about change has been explored.

The Netherlands

The case study which follows is a further example of a training programme for the senior staff of secondary schools which is short in duration but in contrast to the preceding example, its aims are somewhat different. The basic programme provided by the national centre known as *Stichting Gelderse Leergangen* at Arnhem is concerned with 'the school as an organization in a state of change' and while the aim is to develop the individual leader of such an organization, there is also an aim to develop the organization itself. Clearly, therefore, there is some similarity in aims with the training programme developed in Sweden, the main difference being, in the case of the programme in the Netherlands, that the duration is much shorter, namely 13 days spread over a period of about eight months.

Again, some basic information about the educational system in the Netherlands will be given to provide a background to the training programme. The Roman Catholic, Calvinist and Humanist traditions of the Netherlands are mirrored in an educational system which is based on the principles of freedom which emerged from the school struggle of the late 19th and early 20th centuries. Equal status is accorded to all schools based upon the rights of religious and ideological groups. Roughly one third of the schools are Roman Catholic, one third are Protestant and one third are non-denominational. Private schools are subsidized up to 100 per cent by the State. The municipalities receive specific grants for education from central government and act as agents of the central government. As in most other European countries, the educational system in the Netherlands has been undergoing a process of change as a result of new Bills and new Acts which govern education at all levels and especially as a result of the Secondary Education Act of 1963, popularly known as the Mammoth Act, which was enacted in 1968. Since then the Ministry of Education has endeavoured to exercise a stronger influence on the curriculum in an attempt to raise the general level of education and to cope with the needs of minority groups. Primary and secondary education in the Netherlands are clearly separated as regards their teaching staffs and different requirements are made as to their training.

As in other countries the jobs of teachers and of those responsible for schools became more complex and more difficult as the changes in organization took place during the 60s. An enquiry was promised to the Secondary Schools Teachers' Council in 1969 to examine whether teachers' duties had become more onerous through the introduction of the Secondary Education Act. About 3,000 teachers from all branches of secondary education took part in the enquiry during 1970 and 1971 and provided detailed information on the quantity, the nature and the severity of their work. Some of the research findings of the enquiry were as follows.

1. Intensity of the duties
   (a) 24 per cent of the teachers questioned experienced high to very high degrees of stress.
   (b) 33 per cent of teachers replied that they found their work 'a strain' or 'a great strain'. 52 per cent felt that their work was 'rather a strain'.
   (c) As 'reasons for finding their work a strain' 35 per cent attributed the cause of it to 'the children'. 16 per cent mentioned 'renewal' as a reason for finding teaching a strain.

   The investigators concluded that the Secondary Education Act was not the only, and perhaps not the most important, factor making teachers feel that their duties had become more onerous.

2. Differences between heads, assistant heads and other teachers
   (a) Assistant heads were found to have much longer hours. They also spent far more time on general and organizational duties for the benefit of the school than did other staff.
   (b) Heads and assistant heads in progressive schools or experimental schools carried a heavier burden than the rest. Education 'renewal' fell heavily on the shoulders of a relatively small group of teachers including of course, headteachers.

   The researchers expected that the extra duties caused by the introduction of the 'Mammoth Act' would be reduced in the near future for teachers but that, unless special measures were taken, it was likely that the burden on heads and their assistants would increase rather than decrease.

About this time there were many discussions about the training needs of heads and in 1974 a survey was undertaken by AVS, the heads' association, which revealed the need for

urgent action to be taken. The Ministry of Education established a steering group charged with the planning of a training
course for serving heads. This steering group which included
the representatives of teachers and of heads presented a
report—the Giesbers report—which was accepted, and the first
courses began in 1976.

Again the role of central government was significant in
taking national initiatives. There is no doubt that the ready
acceptance of the proposed scheme was due to the interest of
the Minister of Education and to the work of AVS which
provided a driving force behind the development from the
outset.

At the time some of the ways in which the role of the head
had become more difficult in the Netherlands were identified
as follows.

1. Schools had become larger and frequently schools had
   been merged.
2. Many educational innovations were taking place.
3. Forms of administration were becoming more
   complicated.
4. Attitudes to authority were changing.
5. There was insufficient external help for schools.
6. There were increased problems of finance and of space.
7. There was a shift of emphasis from pedagogical—didactic
   matters to problems concerning management.

*The training programme for heads and senior staff in the
Netherlands*

The responsibility for undertaking the training programme
was given to the *Stichting Gelderse Leergangen,* a regional
teacher training centre which runs part-time initial teacher
training and some in-service education. The institution has
links with the Catholic University of Nijmegen where full-time
initial teacher training is provided. It was unusual for a
regional institution to be given a national task but this
probably stems from the fact that Professor J. Giesbers of the
Catholic University of Nijmegen had inspired the early

discussions and the planning of the courses. It was also a fortunate coincidence that the then Minister of Education had been a professor at the same university.

The writer is particularly indebted for details of the courses at Arnhem to his former colleague, Lois Benyon, who attended a course session in 1982, and to Derek Esp who visited Arnhem in 1980.

The training agency has a staff of 12, including a co-ordinator (at the time of writing Dr. Kees J. H. Gielen), eight full-time course leaders, three part-time course leaders and secretarial support. The varied backgrounds of the staff include experience as deputy head of a large secondary school, experience as head of a pedagogical centre, together with social science qualifications, experience in the skills of training adults and commercial management training experience. The basic course in school organization and educational management which is offered at Arnhem is intended for those holding key functions in the management of secondary and tertiary schools. These include heads, deputy heads, heads of departments, co-ordinators and executive administrators. The majority of participants are heads and deputy heads. It is deliberate policy that there are at least two participants from each school taking part, of which it is strongly urged that the head be one. Large schools are permitted to send more than two persons at the same time. Attendance is on a voluntary basis but school boards recommend participants and the Ministry of Education is responsible for all costs. The courses bring together people from all types of secondary schools which is an encouraging feature in a country with a relatively complex educational system involving a considerable variety of ideologies. An attempt is made to form a group for each course which is homogeneous as to size of school. Sub-groups are also formed which are homogeneous according to region and type of school in order to facilitate home-based projects and to enable groups of schools to follow up course sessions. There are usually about 20–24 course members and the number of participants in a year is approximately 480. The courses have usually been oversubscribed. Esp reported that 1,770 members had attended the courses since they started in 1976 and that one head had waited three years before being accepted.

The course is spread over a total of 13 days, which are divided up as follows:

1. There is an initial residential period spent in an hotel.
2. During the following four months, three separate course days are held in the regional sub-groups.
3. The whole course then meets together for a second period of four days in residence.
4. The course is completed by two more separate non-residential course days in regional sub-groups.

There are no qualifications or certifications awarded following the course.

As has been stated already, the aims of the course relate to the changing school and to the role of the senior staff in managing change. The types of change which were reported by heads to Esp have much in common with those reported to the writer by heads in other parts of Western Europe, namely a growing complexity arising from problems of employment legislation and from demands for participation by parents. However, Esp gathered the impression that heads in the Netherlands had a great deal of freedom to manage. Although general staffing establishments are laid down, most heads were engaged in organizational planning within their schools and many of them had powers of staff selection delegated to them. There had been debates on the role of school boards which had emphasized their importance in determining general policy, but these debates also confirmed the need for the board to delegate the execution of the general management to the head. The wider debate on the 'relatively autonomous' school also underlined the key role of the head as pedagogic leader and manager.

An early paper from 1977 states the main objective and the starting point of the courses as 'The development of minimally required knowledge, attitudes and skills that are necessary for a head as leader of an educational organization'. Nor were the aims over-ambitious at this stage, recognizing that given the length of the course (13 days) it could be 'no more than a first step towards solving the problems with which a head is faced daily'.

There was thus a concern with problem-solving from the outset which has remained as a major feature of the courses ever since. In the same paper a number of points were made concerning the methods to be employed.

1. Self-activity: the course members learn through work: a workshop approach was to be adopted.
2. The work of the course must be linked directly with the real school situation.
3. Task-centredness: being a head was to be the starting point of all course activities.
4. Person-centredness: one must be prepared to make one's own functioning as a head a subject for discussion.
5. Experience-centredness: course activities would be based on and related to the everyday experiences of the members.
6. Multiple didactic objectives: the methods and work forms used in the course must be models for the members when they get back into their schools.
7. Flexibility: adjustment of the course or of part of the course must, at all times, be possible.
8. The input of the staff is important but so is that of course members. Both staff and course participants are responsible for the success of the course.

Again, certain features were established which have remained, such as the workshop style with a great deal of group activity and an emphasis on linking the work of the course with the problems of the participants' own schools.

Thomas Van Hees, in a paper presented to the Gatwick conference in 1982, further elaborated the aims as follows:

The aim of the course is to develop knowledge, attitudes, insight and proficiency in the management of a school. The development includes improving:

(a) the ability to tackle problems systematically
(b) the ability to create the structural and psychological conditions necessary for systematic problem-solving by and with the participant's own organization

(c) the participant's insight into his own organization in the process of change
(d) the participant's feelings for co-operative processes in and among groups within his own organization [see ATEE and NAHT, 1982]

It is interesting to note that while problem-solving remains a major preoccupation, other concerns have assumed importance, namely the process of change in an organization and the role of leadership in that process and the understanding of group behaviour. This evolution of the course at Arnhem is further illustrated by the list of subjects dealt with during the course which was given by Van Hees in the same paper:

(a) basic school organization principles
(b) the relation between the educational model and the organizational model
(c) development of the school organization
(d) meeting strategies
(e) change strategies
(f) long-term policy-making
(g) dealing with conflicts
(h) leadership.

There is also clearly now an emphasis on the school as an organization and Benyon (1982) noted a reliance upon the work of Professor E.C.H. Marx of Leyden University in this theoretical area. There is an interesting parallel to be drawn between the development of a concern for leadership of an organization in a process of change and the recent developments in the Swedish programme of school leader training described by Ekholm to the writer.

During the course, participants are given the opportunity of describing and diagnosing the situation in their own schools and of working out solutions to the problems of their own schools. Before the course commences, the participants write a short description of their school and during the first residential session these descriptions are subjected to the scrutiny of other course members in order that they may each gain a number of perceptions of the school and of themselves. At the end of the first residential week the participants re-write their school descriptions, using the information acquired from their discussions and from the methods studied.

Benyon (1982) found that a large part of the first week was devoted to this situational analysis and problem-solving: some nine sessions. She noted with particular interest the method whereby the two representatives from one school, or the 'duo', prepared questions about another school, then separated to question the individual representatives of the second school and subsequently met together to share the perceptions each had gained separately about that school. In like manner, the representatives of the second school acquired perceptions of the first school. The method can only be used, of course, when two representatives from a school attend the course, as is the case in the Netherlands. Benyon further comments,

> The method highlights very easily the problems of collecting facts about schools, the difficulty of formulating questions, the interpretation of the facts in different ways by different people and the constant need to remember that perceptions of an organization differ depending upon where people stand within that organization. (p.3)

During the first residential week there were only three lead lectures and three other sessions were devoted to studying how groups work with the aid of video recordings of group activity.

During the second residential week the course members studied the solution of problems which had been identified in the earlier week and further studied in the home-base at the single-day sessions during the intervening four months. Participants also studied the planning of strategies for change and the role of leadership in the process.

The final two days, in which the sub-groups met again in one of the schools in their area, were devoted to further planning of an action programme for each of their schools.

Following her visit, Benyon concluded that the programme offered at Arnhem was a very professional operation. The regime was a rigorous one for course members: the daily programme began at 9.00 a.m. and ended at 9.30 p.m., and there was little free time. A range of teaching techniques was used including lectures, case studies, video recordings and a great deal of group discussion as well as plenary sessions. Participants were provided with a substantial amount of prescribed reading, including documentation professionally produced at the Centre on such topics as systems analysis, groups within organizations, the diagnosis of conflict and innovation in education. Furthermore, the training team worked very hard for 229 days each year, of which 107 days were contact days with courses. The period of June and July was devoted to preparations for the forthcoming year and thereafter there was a rolling programme of courses for about 500 course members over the year which followed. Benyon sums up:

> by using a variety of methods and by concentrating on only two of the facets of the leader's role, they [the Centre] offer a very professional package. The course has great depth and is handled with great expertise and skill. (p.3)

In 1980 the staff of the Centre were already contemplating further developments of their training programme and what Giesbers described as 'a more far-reaching and continuous schooling for the principals of schools'. They were particularly anxious to develop more advanced and refresher courses and to provide advice and guidance on organizational development in schools. They wished to involve school management teams and indeed whole school staffs in these developments.

One such development was described by Van Hees at Gatwick. It was known as 'System Training in School Organization and Educational Management'. While it is not proposed to describe this programme in detail, brief reference to it will be made because it is a logical development from the basic course in the field of organizational development. These courses are intended for complete 'task groups' in secondary schools, e.g. management teams, project groups or steering groups concerned with the change process. The group consists of at least five and not more than 12 people. Task groups are eligible for this course only if at least two members have attended the basic course. Priority is given to schools which participate in national development projects and schools involved in the formation of communities of schools. The aim of this course is to increase the organizational efficiency of complete 'task groups' of a school in jointly directing or monitoring educational and organizational change in their own institution. The courses are designed to match the needs of the group and of the school in question and examples of changes which might be under consideration were given as follows:

(a) the preparation for reorganization as a community of schools or for a merger of two or more schools
(b) the preparation for growth or for the gradual winding-up and closure of a school
(c) the setting-up of a new decision-making structure
(d) the evaluation of the existing communication in a school and its improvement.

The course is primarily of a workshop nature and the work done is based exclusively on the participants' own situations. The knowledge required is obtained as much as possible through individual studies. The course covers a total of seven working days and is divided as follows:

- a working meeting at the participants' school for programming the course
- a two-day conference at a conference centre
- three working meetings at the participants' school
- a two-day conference at a conference centre
- two working meetings at the participants' own school.

Working meetings in principle last half a day. The total programme, including individual study and the performance of tasks, requires about ten days. 12 schools can participate in this programme per year. (p. 22).

The training team has attempted various evaluations of its work. During the first year (1976–77) questionnaires were sent out before the course began asking participants to indicate priorities and problems which they would like to be dealt with during the course. This suggested that it would be possible to devote the necessary attention to all problems and the practice was discontinued because of unfavourable student reaction.

Since then various techniques have been used to discover how participants react to content and presentation of the various sections of the programme. The present co-ordinator, Kees Gielen, commented to Esp that feedback is useful for course planning but notes that 'over-much evaluation irritates the participants if there is no change', (Esp, 1980). Conversely, a good atmosphere on a course may lead to absence of criticism.

The co-ordinator also reported to Esp that he was very conscious of the limitations imposed by lack of time, lack of sufficient staff and by financial restrictions. He would have liked to add a consultant in organizational development to his team. He saw a need to train the members of local school boards, for more school-based training and for more follow-up to the basic course. He recognized that the programme offered an 'emergency kit' and that training needed to be extended. This could require additional funding.

Heads and deputies whom Esp met during his visit spoke favourably of the training. It had recognition and national status and had practical relevance to their work and to the problems confronting them in their schools. The residential element was costly but was necessary to achieve isolation from day-to-day pressures. It also developed the ethos and cohesion of a group and strengthened links with other heads which continued beyond the period of the course.

There was some criticism that the course did not deal adequately with industrial relations which were becoming more difficult, with conflict situations and with the increasing demands for democratic participation. The Catholic Pedagogic Centre expressed the need to complete the basic training of all 3,000 heads of general and technical secondary schools as soon as possible and to proceed to develop team training and school-focused training: 'People need consultation throughout the whole process of change'.

This comment highlights what is perhaps the greatest problem facing the training team at Arnhem, a problem of which they are well aware. Resource difficulties prevent the trainers from following through the developments in schools which they help to initiate. Trainers are not able to attend all non-residential day sessions and although schools benefit from exchanging information and experiences, they do not necessarily follow their priority tasks through but concentrate upon 'safer' and less contentious issues while they do not have consultant help in the school. As is being learned slowly in other countries, particularly in Sweden, it takes a long time to change attitudes, to learn new skills and to follow changes in schools through. It seems unlikely that these changes can be achieved by short courses alone without some immediate support or follow-up, either in the form of a further course for the 'task group' as outlined above or by the provision of consultant help in the school. Some schools are able to sustain their own momentum of change by distinguished leadership and by school-based or school-focused training but most hard-pressed heads would value some help from outside. This need for more time and for continued support for developments in the schools is perhaps the main drawback to the course at Arnhem. However, this is not to underestimate the value of the ambitious and very professional initiative which has been successfully developed by the team which is working there.

Esp expressed his enthusiasm for what is happening in these terms: 'The Arnhem courses provide an excellent opportunity for heads and put the Netherlands in the premier league of European headteacher training initiatives'. (p.15).

Norway

This final case-study is taken from Norway and describes the programme which has now been adopted as a national scheme for training the heads and the senior staff of the basic compulsory school, or *grunnskole*. This school provides a nine-year period of education for children from age seven to 16. The training scheme is known by the title *'Miljø og Ledelse i Skolen'*, the translation of which into English is perhaps 'The working environment and the running of the school'. By the 'working environment' is meant the working conditions, the situation in and around the school and the climate and atmosphere of the school. What distinguishes the Norwegian programme from others is that it sets out to provide a course of leadership training but to set this training against the background of the school. Thus it aims to provide for the development of individual leaders and also to promote the development of their schools. The training course for the heads and for others is seen as an integral part of an organizational development programme for schools. The Norwegians have recognized that this process takes a considerable period of time and the programme now extends over some three years. This pattern of training has evolved from a variety of initiatives and experiments which have been carried out by a number of different institutions in Norway and the writer is particularly indebted to the following individuals for providing him with details of these developments. Oddvar Vormeland, Director of Education, Oslo and Akershus, has been chairman of the National Council for Compulsory Education which co-ordinates and partially funds the national training pro-gramme. He directed the Council of Europe Seminar 'Current trends in school management' in Kristiansand in 1982 and is still closely associated with the national programme. Per Kvist, Director of Education in the County of Hordaland, is also chairman of the National Council of Innovation in Education and his work has greatly influenced the shape of the national training programme. He contributed a paper on this work to the Gatwick Conference. Sigrid Kjos-Hansen contri-buted a paper on developments in Trondheim to the seminar at Kristiansand (1982) and Wayne Flynn of Oregon, USA also contributed an influential paper at the same conference. He also carried out a preliminary evaluation of the Norwegian training programme.

The Norwegian education system has evolved in a highly centralized form because of a need to provide equal opportunities for people living in varying geographical and social circumstances in a country where a significant number of people live in remote rural areas. As early as the middle of the 12th century, education was provided in the 'learned schools' which were run by the clergy, and provision for compulsory, basic education has existed in Norway since the middle of the 18th century. Compulsory schooling for seven years' duration has existed in Norway since 1889. The Ministry of Cultural and Scientific Affairs lays down minimum standards for work, equipment, buildings, teaching aids, floor space and class sizes, and at school level approves all text books and controls the curriculum. Increasingly, however, administration is being devolved to regional and local boards. The *grunnskole* is administered by local boards. Norway is divided into 18 counties and each county has a Director of Education who supervises the work of the boards. The most recent developments in the *grunnskole* originated from the model plan for the compulsory school, known as the Mønster Plan, or M74 which was drawn up in 1969 and after passing through evolutionary stages was officially adopted in 1974. Under this plan greater autonomy was given to local communities to play a more active role in determining the education of young people in the community. The plan also stressed that the principle of co-operation between teacher, pupil and home governed the task of the compulsory school. Co-operation between teachers and pupils was to serve as a model for teaching democratic ideas and practices. The working methods at the school were to emphasize co-operation and participation. New bodies for such co-operation were established under the Mønster Plan, including the pupils' council, the parents' council, the teachers' council, the council for employees other than teachers and a co-ordinating committee where all members of the school community were represented.

The creation of all these new groups, which were being given influential roles in the direction of local schools, has had significant implications for the role of the head in Norway. Clearly, the head occupied a focal position at the centre of these various interacting forces and if they were to be woven together into a cohesive unit yet each enabled to fulfil their own roles, a heavy responsibility rested on the head. Heads were also going to experience greatly increased pressures both from inside and from outside the school. If people were to learn to work co-operatively together, negotiation had to take place which would enable group members to function collaboratively in the groups to which they belonged and also to solve problems jointly and to make decisions. In the local setting it was the head who was viewed as having the time and possessing the legitimate authority to perform this vital co-ordinating and leadership function. Among the details of the head's role as laid down in the *Handbok for Skolen Del 1,* the head is described as the pedagogical and administrative leader of the school. He is responsible for creating a good pedagogical environment within the school and for making pedagogical development work possible. Some of the duties which are relevant to the new responsibilities mentioned above are as follows:

1. To administer the school according to the law, the instructions for the compulsory school and the decisions made by the local school board.
2. To work to further prosperity and collaboration between all those who are linked to the school.
3. To be responsible for planning, information and consultation at the school.
4. To see that collaborative boards are formed, to see that conditions at the school are dealt with by these boards, and that newly elected representatives get information about the boards and their fields of work.
5. To see that meetings between the parents of a class and the class teacher, as well as such meetings for the whole school, are held according to a plan made in co-operation with the teachers at the school.
6. To arrange conditions for social activities and varied spare time activities with the collaboration board.
7. To work out budget estimates in co-operation with the school's boards and to see that the grants are spent in a suitable way.

Clearly, these duties relate to the responsibilities placed upon the head both to set up appropriate 'collaborative' structures for decision-making and to see that these groups, once set up, function properly. In the past the work of a school had been much more restricted and the head's role was concerned with carrying out directions from a central authority. Under these circumstances the need for training was less obvious, and heads received little specialized training for their administrative duties. With the advent of the Mønster Plan the role of the head changed significantly. The role was expanded to include wider responsibilities, as has been illustrated and these responsibilities demanded both knowledge and skills with which they had not been equipped, in the course of their previous careers as teachers. They were also called upon to exercise more initiative and creativity than had formerly been the case. In other words, the Norwegian head was experiencing in the mid-1970s many of the problems faced by other European colleagues, but in the demands for participation from both inside and outside the school, supported by the force of law, those problems probably presented themselves in a more acute form.

Flynn (1982) points out some of the problems facing the Norwegian head. The new role expectations made it necessary to play an influential role and the traditional role of the head in Norway had not endowed the possessor with significant influence. He did not play a strong role in appointing or dismissing staff. He did not evaluate staff performance formally and his influence in the areas of reward or coercion was not great. Thus, the role of head had not been perceived as a highly influential one and the legitimate influence derived from the role was not high. Flynn suggests that given the leadership role expected by the Mønster Plan, 'expert' knowledge and skills are necessary for heads in the fields of human relationships, communications, group dynamics, problem-solving, conflict management and decision-making. A well-organized training programme was necessary to include all these elements. While some heads would be able to exert the necessary influence and command respect by the force of their personalities, most heads would need help to achieve this in a country with a strong democratic tradition and in which the concepts of 'power' and of 'the expert' are looked upon with a degree of scepticism. There is a splendid Norwegian saying that 'An expert is a very ordinary man who is a very long way from home'.

One of the results of these trends, reported by Derek Esp, following a visit to Norway in 1980, was that recruitment for headship was slowing down. He gives as one of the reasons for this the increasing need for heads to exercise democratic leadership. He also noted other factors such as low salary differentials and taxation patterns. There appeared to be no accepted ladder of promotion although experience as a deputy or as a school counsellor was an advantage.

Some training for heads began as early as the mid 60s. It took the form mainly of providing information in lecture form. The need to provide more appropriate training for the heads of *grunnskole* was recognized during the late 70s and a number of initiatives were being taken by different organizations. There seemed to be a general recognition of the need for short courses dealing with administrative processes, the law and budgeting but also a need for basic courses concerned with attitudes, communications, and the resolving of conflicts. Geography and other factors seemed to underline the need to provide a variety of solutions to meet the needs of very different regions. However, by 1977 some people were beginning to express dissatisfaction with the traditional course in which the head was withdrawn from the school, trained and then returned to the school. Oddvar Vormeland comments on the 'need to work on "the inner life" of the school—to link the aims and the daily work'.

Per Kvist reports the increased emphasis on the leadership role of heads and the importance of interpersonal relationships in training for leadership in his booklet 'Working Conditions and Leadership in Schools' (AMS) 1982: 'The objective was to involve the whole staff in making decisions and sharing responsibility, to help schools to adjust to the new situation and to bring about innovation'. Kvist and his colleagues were coming to the conclusion that modifications to traditional courses did not have the effect of involving the school staff in any proposed changes.

> It was difficult to carry the contents of the courses into effect in the schools. There are various reasons, one of them being the common resistance to change. People resist changes for the sake of change alone. The staffs were not involved in the issues at stake and could not really be expected to pay much attention to the process of innovation. The general conclusion was that the staff and the head must be involved in the process of development at the same time. (p. 1).

While traditional courses had been held for many years in a county like Hordaland, it had been discovered that when the head was trained alone and away from the school, there was little evidence of any transfer of benefit back to the school. This was an important conclusion and is the background philosophy to the project known as *Miljø og Ledelse (AMS)*, whereby the training of the leader is linked with and happens alongside the development of the school and involves the staff of the school. This became the model for the national programme for training heads and senior staff in Norway and will be described in some detail as it happens in the county of Hordaland.

However, reference must be made to another organization which has influenced the development of the Norwegian programme, and that is International Movements Towards Educational Change, or IMTEC. This private organization has its international headquarters in Oslo. The organization was originally established in the early 1970s as a project of the Organization for Economic Cooperation and Development (OECD) for the purpose of studying and promoting educational change. More recently it has become an independent organization and continues to provide consultancy services for individuals and for institutions throughout the world, helping them to define, initiate and carry out educational innovations. The director of IMTEC is Per Dalin, who made a significant contribution to the Windsor workshop. IMTEC has as the basis of its programme the belief that 'any changes must find a basis in real needs of students, teachers, administrators and the local environment; solutions to problems need to be experienced and "owned" by the actors themselves'.

Work in Norway—for example, in the region of Trondheim—was used to refine the Institutional Development Programme offered by IMTEC. One feature of this approach to organizational development is the involvement of the whole staff in a situational analysis which is to serve as a 'base line' for establishing the priorities for development in a school. An instrument in the form of a questionnaire is completed by the whole staff anonymously for this purpose. A second feature of this programme is the use of external consultants to support the school during a period of development. It would not be appropriate to give a fuller account here of the work of IMTEC, which has a much wider international setting, but the particular approach to organizational development which it has evolved and the use of external consultants have influenced the development of the training programme in Norway and helped to give it a distinctive character compared with other programmes in Western Europe. A number of counties in Norway have employed the services of IMTEC in developing their training programmes and Sigrid Kjos-Hansen described at Kristiansand a programme in the region of Trondheim which had taken advantage of those services for the training of consultants. Of course the county in question has to fund the additional expense of paying for such services.

The national programme for training heads and senior staff of grunnskole: Miljø og Ledelse i Skolen

This programme is the first nationwide attempt to provide an in-service training for the senior staff of schools on a systematic basis in Norway. The programme is co-ordinated centrally by a steering committee of the National Council for Compulsory Education. There is also a 'reference' or advisory group which includes a wide representation of the teachers' and parents' associations as well as other interested parties. The Council is partly responsible for the funding of the programme, which was launched in 1981 for a period of three years in the first instance. A further period of three years is now being budgeted for, and by the end of that period, that is in 1986, it is hoped that some 50 per cent of heads and schools will have had experience of the scheme.

The training programme itself takes place in the regions and is the responsibility of the Director of Education in each of the 18 counties which are now all taking part in the scheme. Half the cost of the programme is borne by the local communities and half comes from central funds. The programme is divided into three parts, extending over a period of some three years.

A First there is a basic course of five days' duration which is intended mainly for newly appointed heads. These days are spread over half a year and the participants are expected to study in between the single days. The topics dealt with during these days are legislation, the structure of the school system, economy, school law, information and planning, cooperation, pupils' rights and office routines. This is a 'first aid' or 'survival kit' for new heads.

B The second stage is the most extensive part of the programme. It extends over a total of 15 days which are spread over one and a half years. These days are divided up into seminars of varying lengths, that is, they may be two or three days long. This course deals with leadership training and with school development. A more detailed account of a specific example of such a B course will be given for the County of Hordaland.

C The third stage is a follow-up course lasting from one to three days. It is meant to provide an opportunity for exchanging experiences and for gaining new ideas and new inspiration to maintain the processes which were initiated during the B course.

A useful handbook for those concerned with the national programme was produced by the project leader Terje Seljelid in 1982. As well as outlining the ideological background to the project 'The working environment and the running of the school' it provides valuable guidelines on all aspects of the programme for those taking part, including the timetable, the content and the methods which may be found to be effective. Particular attention is directed to the work which is to be carried out in the schools and there is emphasis on the continuous nature of development in contemporary schools. Development is unlikely to be completed within the periods allocated to Parts A and B of the programme.

Neither the training of the school administrators nor the work with the school can be considered as adequate and complete within the time-limit. The problems and challenges change and will continue to do so. So completion of courses A and B cannot be seen as a satisfactory and complete form of in-service training. For many schools course B will only be a preparation or beginning of the work. (p.40).

The statement represents a similar conclusion to that

gradually being arrived at elsewhere, particularly in Sweden, that changes in schools take a long time and three years may be an insufficient time in some instances.

The training programme in the County of Hordaland

The training programme in the County of Hordaland has been going on since 1978 when it started as an experimental project, jointly funded by the County and by the National Council for Innovation in Education. It has been well documented by the Director of Education (Per Kvist) and there has been some evaluation of the scheme. It was originally established to implement comprehensive education and so has a background concern with facilitating change.

The county of Hordaland includes the city of Bergen and has a population of 250,000. There are 400 *grunnskole* and half of these schools are in Bergen itself. The rest are in muncipalities of very varied size. For example, one municipality covering a large geographical area has a total population of 200 and 30 pupils of compulsory school age. Teaching staff of *grunnskole* range from three to 50.

The training programme in Hordaland will serve as a good example particularly of the B Course as it came into the national scheme with a well-developed model which has not had to be substantially modified, although some changes had taken place, following the inception of the experimental project. By 1982 some 100 schools all over the county were involved in the programme and there was co-operation with the teachers' training colleges in Bergen and at Stord where some evaluation of the programme had been undertaken.

The principles of the training programme in Hordaland are set out as follows in Per Kvist's booklet (1982):

1. Leadership is a comprehensive concept. Superintendents, heads and teachers are all leaders and need leadership training. Heads are key figures in schools and therefore strategies for change and innovation should take particular care to secure their full involvement and co-operation.

117

2. The training should be organized in such a way that leadership, change and innovation are continually subject to discussion in the school community.
3. There should be widespread participation by the people involved at all levels of the project. Responsibility for progress lies within the school, not outside.
4. The innovation process should start on the basis of a self-analytical diagnosis and be problem-oriented.
5. Key personnel, consultants and project leaders should be given adequate training. The focus should be on stimulating *processes* for change in schools, and on transferring instruments and techniques for effective problem-solving to schools, which should enable them to build a process of self-renewal.
6. The project should be subject to continuous evaluation. (p.2).

Participation in the programme is on a voluntary basis. If a school wishes to participate, it may only do so provided that a majority of the staff agrees. There are two parts to this B course:

1. Initiation of the process of innovation at the individual school.
2. Training the head and one teacher from each school at a special course in leadership.

The priority given to innovation is significant and in his paper presented at Gatwick Per Kvist expressed it thus:

When considering the B course, it must be stated that the innovation process at the individual school is the main thing. The training programme for head teachers and for other key figures is designed to help them become change agents in their schools' efforts towards educational development.

The course lasts for two years, of which one half-year is devoted to information and preparation.

ORGANIZATION

1. The central decision-making group managing the programme consists of:
   - the Director of Education in Hordaland as project leader,
   - the municipal school-director in Bergen,
   - the deans of the two teachers' training colleges in the county.
2. The administration group consists of three administrators from the Director of Education's office and one from the municipal school office in Bergen.
3. There are local management groups, one in each region, having responsibility for practical arrangements.
4. A planning group is formed in each participant school, composed of the head and two elected members of staff.
5. A 'reference' or advisory group is formed consisting of elected representatives, heads, teachers, teachers' training colleges, the University of Bergen, teachers' associations and professionals in relevant fields of education.

A BRIEF DESCRIPTION OF THE PROGRAMME

TIMING
The programme extends over a period of more than two years.

Year 1, autumn: Information
          spring: Preparation
Year 2, autumn: Implementation
          spring: Implementation (continued)
Year 3, autumn: Conclusion

INFORMATION
During this period of half a year the schools in a district receive information about the programme in two ways: (a) through leaflets and other information designed for the project, and (b) through visits to the schools by representatives of the local school authorities who attend staff meetings. The staff makes a decision to join or not to join the programme by a majority vote. The implication of joining the programme is that the head and one teacher from the staff are obliged to join the leadership training programme.

PREPARATION

Schools voting to participate in the programme start making preparations.

(a) The planning group for managing and leading the innovation work in the school is elected by the staff. This group is normally composed of the head and two other elected members of the staff. During the preparation period this group meets other groups from the school district to discuss practical issues and strategies for change in schools.

(b) One teacher is elected to attend the leadership training programme together with the head.

(c) 'Study groups' for the leadership training programme are organized in different districts. Each group is composed of two participants from three schools, i.e. 6 persons. Often personnel from the local school administration will join the study groups too. All study groups in a district will hold a seminar during the preparation time for discussion of materials and strategies.

(d) Two consultants are appointed to each group. The consultants work with the study groups and follow the innovation process in the schools represented in their group. They also work closely with the planning groups of individual schools. The consultants are paid by the local school authorities.

(e) School staffs have structured discussions about 'the hidden curriculum' and 'school climate'. This has proved helpful in preparing staffs mentally for innovation and enables them to look beyond the solution of mere practical problems and consider innovation in a wider perspective. The work is co-ordinated to take place during the staff's allocation of planning time which, at present, amounts to 40 hours per year.

(f) Plans for using time and other resources for implementing the programme during the following year are prepared and decided by each participating school.

IMPLEMENTATION

Work in the schools begins with the completion of an

instrument for situational analysis by all members of the staff. The instrument is divided into three parts:

(i) The diagnosis of the current situation.
(ii) The identification of goals for the school.
(iii) The planning proposals for strategies to achieve the proposed goals.

This instrument was devised by a local group and has much in common with other instruments used in organizational development. The consultants usually administer this instrument in cooperation with the school's planning group. The analysis has six different items:

1. Educational tasks and ways of working.
2. Cooperation between teachers and planning of work.
3. Decision-making.
4. The situation of the pupils.
5. School and home.
6. The framework within which the school must operate.

This analysis helps schools to become conscious of the 'climate' of the school and of the varied perceptions of the school by its members. A priority list of problems is drawn up which reveals the major concerns of the staff. According to their interests the staff form working groups to tackle the priority problems which are agreed upon. A time-table for working on these problems is agreed upon. The planning group co-ordinates this work and supports the groups in their problem-solving throughout the year. The consultant provides help where it is appropriate.

During the year the whole staff may go away for a two to three-day seminar to discuss their problems, and concentrate on the process of innovation. These seminars are valuable for developing human relationships among the staff and are subsidized from county resources. (In addition to the 40 hours' planning time being devoted to this programme, some schools have managed to give the planning group and other groups involved in time-consuming activities some compensation in the form of reduced teaching time or extra wages). Some examples of the tasks undertaken by groups in schools in Hordaland as part of the training programme are as follows:

- developing different ways of working together and developing the 'climate' for co-operation and team-work
- improving communication between teachers and pupils
- involving pupils and parents in decorating the school or improving the playgrounds
- enabling staff to influence the 'climate' by studying rules, regulations and the resources available
- improving relationships between home and school.

More recently, the emphasis has shifted from 'co-operation between teachers and planning of work' to 'co-operation in the classroom and educational development as major themes'.

THE LEADERSHIP TRAINING PROGRAMMES

The participants in the leadership training programme are the head and one teacher from each participant school together with local school administrators. Participants from three schools form a study group. Six study groups form a regional group. Local school administrators will join one of the groups belonging to their region. Study groups also include consultants.

The training programme consists of six major themes:

1. Implementing the objectives of the school.
2. Communications and human relations.
3. Conflict and problem-solving.
4. Co-operation in the classroom and educational development.
5. Roles of leadership at different levels of the school system.
6. Influencing decisions and sharing responsibility.

Study groups concentrate on one of the major themes each, in order to present this to the other groups at the regular regional seminars. There are six such seminars during the study year and each seminar lasts for two days. There is a social evening to open each seminar and this has proved to be of value in developing a group feeling or atmosphere.

Taking responsibility for the presentation of one of the major themes at one of the seminars is a 'must' for every group. Otherwise, groups are free to take up other sub-themes or study whatever other theme they find relevant.

CONSULTANTS

The programme clearly demands a large number of consultants on the basis that two consultants are allocated to three schools. In 1981, 25 consultants were needed. Some consultants are teachers, some are psychologists, some lecturers at teachers' training colleges; a few are heads or school administrators.

Much thought has been given to the role and training of consultants in Hordaland. The role makes considerable demands because the consultants are rarely professional consultants and usually have another main job. Also although they may be very enthusiastic, they may not have appropriate training and experience. Some help has been gained from commercial organizations in Norway, e.g. from IMTEC, from the training colleges, from advisers or from colleagues in other schools. While consultants are not expected to be omniscient, they must have credibility with the school and have a sound theoretical training and ability in various techniques. Kvist expresses the role of the consultant thus:

> The consultants will not try to solve the problems or take part in arguments, but they will try to help the staff solve their own problems and encourage the process of change in the school. Also they are a channel of communication to resources outside the school, such as people and literature.

A great deal of expertise in the field of human relationships as well as a large amount of time is required of consultants. They also need to observe confidentiality if schools are to be prepared to share problems in threatening areas with confidence and to develop an openness in their negotiations. Training is now provided for all consultants in Hordaland. They attend all sessions of the leadership training programme for 'their' schools and in addition have ten days' training which runs concurrently with the training programme. Two training sessions take place before the consultant meets the school team. The training for the consultant includes learning about non-directive counselling techniques and training methods. Training during the programme offers opportunities for consultants to share in case-work discussions based upon their current work in the schools.

Consultants have the difficult task of holding up a 'mirror' to the school and reflecting an independent and non-judgmental perception of the school to its members, leaving them free to determine the school's development but equally free to seek further help should they desire it.

The introduction of the consultant into a programme for training heads is one of the outstanding features of the Norwegian training scheme and one which distinguishes this programme from others in Western Europe. Clearly the success of the enterprise may well depend upon the recruitment of a substantial body of consultants who are sensitive, skilled and highly trained. However, once such a body of consultants has been built up, it will represent an enormous national and regional resource for promoting and supporting school development. Meanwhile, the Norwegians are developing a particular area of expertise from which others may learn much.

EVALUATION

There has been evaluation of the training programme in Hordaland both by the course organizers using the now usual administration of questionnaires, and also by an independent team working at the Stord College of Education.

The final report on the latter enquiry is not available at the time of writing but a summary of interim findings written by Ivar Njerve was presented to the Windsor workshop. These represent preliminary impressions rather than final conclusions. The purposes of this study were

1. To evaluate the training programme through the participants' own views about its value. A questionnaire was used with a random sample of 30 participants.
2. To estimate the effect of innovation work in 13 individual schools selected at random. A case study

method was used, the schools being studied for one and a half years, and a variety of methods was used in the collection of data.

The work was carried out during the period 1980–83. Some of the preliminary impressions of the study are as follows.

1. INDIVIDUAL OUTCOMES
   1. All participants agree that it is a great advantage that heads and teachers take part in the training programme together.
   2. Many participants think that the training has changed their professional role. They feel that they have become more democratic, more sensitive, more liable to change their attitudes and be more considerate to others.
   3. Most participants find the contents have been relevant and topical. Issues such as communication, the role of leadership and problem-solving are particularly mentioned.
   4. A large number of teachers when interviewed expressed a lack of interest in solving social problems or discussing questions of communication. Their need for renewal was more concerned with methods of teaching. They considered that the training had not sufficiently emphasized the function of the head as professional and pedagogical leader of the school. Neither was it demonstrated how a process of development or renewal could be created within the school itself.

2. SCHOOL OUTCOMES
   1. Transferring knowledge and skills from leadership training to individual schools is a difficult problem. Many participants claim that this would be easier if a larger number of teachers from each school took part in the programme.
   2. The most common obstacles to transferring ideas from the programme to the school are shortage of time and of money. However, most participants think

125

also that positive personal resources such as interest and enthusiasm can make up for such obstacles.

3. At more than half the schools most teachers say that positive changes in 'climate' have taken place as a result of participation in the programme. The changes that are mentioned most frequently are more teamwork, more openness among teachers and between teaching staff and administration, or the achievement of practical projects such as improving the playground, decorating the school buildings or simplifying the school regulations.

4. Surprisingly, many teachers had only vague ideas about the aim and contents of the programme that their school was taking part in. They referred to lack of information and had experienced very little as a concrete result of the course.

5. The head's influence on how the school worked with the programme was considerable. Wherever a head was negative or passive the effect of the programme was minimal. It was important that the head took an active part in the programme, right from the beginning, not only taking part in discussions but also in the practical execution of decisions and in procuring human and material resources for the programme.

Schools in Contact (SIK)

'Schools in Contact' (SIK) is a follow-up project which has been developed in Hordaland. All schools which have participated in the initial (AMS) programme are offered the opportunity to take part in the follow-up programme. Those schools which join this programme are able to continue the innovation process with support from outside agencies (including consultants) for another year or two.

The title of the project is somewhat misleading as the original idea was that schools in a district which had attended the initial (AMS) programme would co-operate and support each other in furthering the process of change. The geographical extent of the county of Hordaland has rendered this very difficult to achieve although there are exceptions.

Schools voting to join the follow-up scheme elect a new planning-group of three persons. It is regarded as an advantage that the head remains a member of this group. The school may choose whether or not to have a consultant. In contrast to AMS, the SIK programme offers one consultant per school.

The school again uses an instrument of diagnosis and goes through the process of analysis, defining its problems and setting its priorities. Schools are invited to take part in one-day seminars twice a year to discuss their problems and to share experiences. These seminars provide an opportunity of contact and co-operation between different schools and are particularly useful for giving the planning group a new impetus. In 1982, out of 34 schools which had taken part in AMS, 23 schools or 68 per cent voted to join SIK. In 1981 there were 83 schools taking part in SIK, 42 of them with consultants.

Conclusions

The national programme which has evolved in Norway following a number of individual regional initiatives, developed over a period of some ten years, is the fruit of considerable experience in the field and seems to combine many of those features of training which are particularly relevant to schools at this time in Western Europe.

The crucial role of the head and the need for training is recognized but the inclusion of a second member of the staff introduces another perception of the school. The head is not the only leader. There is specific leadership training for two members of each school staff with emphasis on their roles as change agents. Secondly, change is recognized as a fact of school life and therefore an attempt is made to integrate the training in leadership with the organizational development of the school. The intention is to involve the whole staff of the school in the training programme. This is manifestly difficult to achieve and the strategy of offering the services of external consultants to support schools which are going through developmental processes is a further positive step.

Such a programme deserves the closest attention from those

who see the need for leadership in conditions of change as a major problem facing schools in Western Europe today.

CHAPTER 4

Some Issues of Training Methodology

Very little is known about the behaviour or motivation of heads, principals or experienced administrators in a learning situation, or about the teaching methods which are most likely to be effective for their training. The age range may be between 35 and 60 and, as had been noted in a quotation from Mats Ekholm, the empirical knowledge which we possess on the developmental psychology of adults in this age-range is not impressive. For some the experience of a return to the learning situation after a considerable period of time may be daunting. All will share a feeling of some uncertainty, even those who are mature and confident. The range of expectations which they bring with them will vary widely, from eager anticipation to deep suspicion. The range of experience and backgrounds from which they come will provide a rich resource on the one hand but, on the other, may pose many problems to the providers in determining what is the most appropriate methodology to employ. It is not possible within the scope of this study to explore the issues of adult learning in any depth but this chapter will examine some of the practical problems which confront programme organizers in this area and will indicate some of the lessons which are emerging from current practice in various countries.

Training methods

The difficulties and uncertainties surrounding the development of appropriate training methods and the inadequacy of certain methods in current use are generally recognized. The first two conclusions of the Windsor workshop, from the evidence of research, were that:

(a) there is no one best way of training school leaders, and
(b) many existing courses do not change the actual behaviour of the school leader.

In the absence of any well-established and generally accepted methodology, a wide variety of methods are in use in Europe at present. Participants at the Windsor workshop recognized this diversity and proposed that a number of different methods, none of them mutually exclusive, needed to be further tried and tested. These were:

1. individual support for the head
2. small group work with other heads
3. training of the head and another member of staff outside the school
4. developmental work with the whole staff of the school
5. developmental work involving a school, its community and its governing body.

They also stressed that in the present economic climate it was important that school leaders and their staffs should take as much responsibility as possible for their own further development, thus retaining ownership of their own learning and tailoring training to meet their individual needs. The method was cost-effective and the scale of need for training was so great that no country could afford to mount too many labour-intensive courses.

The area in which the widest diversity of methodology exists may be described as the 'ideological divide' between those programmes which are concerned to equip the individual with qualities necessary to be an effective leader and those programmes which, while developing the individual, are more concerned with the development of the school and with the role of the individual as a change-agent in bringing about that development. Both approaches have been illustrated and they represent, for the most part, different methodologies. The latter approach tends to put much greater emphasis upon the use of the 'real' situation of the school as the environment for learning, as in the case of the Swedish programme, whereas the former approach which takes place away from the school, as in France, makes more use of teaching materials such as case studies and simulations.

Reference has already been made to the 'lively debate' which took place in the PLUS commission on how the interaction between theory and practice should be organized within the Swedish training programmes. One view was that by working through a number of simulated situations the school leaders were expected to obtain an improved readiness to act in future situations. The other line of argument maintained that the point of departure should instead be the concrete and immediate experiences and problems that each participant brought with him from his own everyday situation. In the event, the latter view prevailed in Sweden and has profoundly influenced training in that country.

However, the debate has continued elsewhere and is certainly not resolved in favour of one particular approach or the other; in fact there is perhaps a growing belief that such methods are not mutually exclusive. For example, in the Norwegian programme outlined in the previous chapter, both approaches have their place.

Not unrelated to the foregoing is the discussion on the relative parts to be played by theory and practice in training programmes for school leaders. It is the experience of the writer both from participation in the running of the courses in England and from more recent meetings with providers in other countries that in this area, course organizers face a considerable dilemma. In general, one encounters among school leaders a suspicion of theory and of those who come from an academic background. Participants in such training programmes almost always seem to favour a methodology which relates directly to the practical problems of running schools. Clive Hopes reported to the Gatwick conference (see ATEE and NAHT, 1982) that in the Federal Republic of Germany

Trainers experience strong resistance to theoretical

concepts by those who are practice-oriented. In the development of training programmes for practitioners, researchers have been forced to draw upon experiences from other fields where management training is practised ... The theory which has been generated in these fields sometimes appears literally foreign to the target group, not only because of irritating jargon, but also because of its apparent unrelatedness to the practitioners' day-to-day environment.

The research or 'theory-oriented' trainer may lack experience within the school system and, moreover, may not have devoted adequate time to developing practical examples drawn from the practitioners' world, which might illustrate the concepts. However, it cannot be denied that there is a need for a conceptual input into training programmes, otherwise there is a danger that they will degenerate into the provision of 'practical tips' or explanations of 'how the system works'. It is the experience of the writer that course organizers walk a tightrope in this area and he has found it prudent to adopt the method of moving from practice to principle rather than the other way round. The evaluation of the training programme in Northern Ireland which was carried out by Sister Anne O'Shea (1983) and which is described in more detail in the following chapter illustrates this problem and comes out strongly for a similar strategy, quoting one of the participants as saying:

> The abstract discussion of theoretical issues must not predominate. Discussion must focus on practical issues ... Discussion should move from the concrete to the abstract, not from the abstract to the nebulous. (p.32).

In France, the Commission chaired by de Peretti on the training of teachers suggests a number of valuable principles for the establishment of a 'theory of practice' in the field of adult learning, arguing that such training at present is insufficiently practical and far too academic. Some of those principles are as follows:

1. Training should observe the principles of appropriateness and realism.

2. Training should begin with the people being trained: their experience, their needs, their preoccupations and their problems.
3. Transfer of learning should not be left to the clients.
4. The practical aspects of training should be prepared with great care.
5. Provision should be made for alternating practice with reflection throughout the period of training.
6. Training programmes should be flexible and adaptable to needs, allowing learners to participate in designing programmes, to suggest areas of experiment and to engage in action research. (de Peretti, 1982).

A 'theory of practice' implies the development of a theoretical base to the learning of skills: a conceptualization of practice in such areas as observation and enquiry, analysis, formative evaluation, the theory of group interaction and the psychology of counselling (p. 113).

An attempt is thus being made to achieve a better match between theory and practice in the training programmes in France and in so doing is shifting the emphasis from cognitive learning to the acquisition of skills. This represents an important development in the search for an appropriate methodology for the training of principals and other school leaders. Consequently, the reasons given for lengthening the training period from three months to one year are in order to provide more opportunity for practical experience in schools and also to provide for the study in greater depth of such topics as group dynamics, the analysis of institutions, formative evaluation, comparative studies and adolescent psychology (p.190).

Other countries may not have expressed their aims and intentions in such formal terms as in France but nevertheless there is an evident trend towards the development of methods which are experiential rather than simply cognitive. This trend is closely related to the movement noted earlier in this study towards emphasizing the importance of learning skills as well as acquiring knowledge or information. Mintzberg's analogy of the swimmer has already been quoted. Skills are acquired by practice followed by feed-back.

133

Two illustrations from different European countries may serve to illustrate this trend as it penetrates educational management.

Terje Seljelid, the project leader for the Norwegian national training programme 'The working environment and the running of the school', has written a handbook (1982) for those concerned with the programme, which provides useful guidance on training methods. The writer advises trainers to use a variety of methods and in particular to use 'process-experiencing' methods as well as 'lecture-discussion in plenary sessions'. He further advocates 'a conscious combination of the two methods' as the best 'single' way of working. However, he issues a cautionary word that to use the process-experiencing method it is necessary for a course leader or group discussion leader to be not only well trained in this type of work but also to know about and thoroughly understand the mental and social processes at work. Given this condition, however, 'Experiencing social processes in a course situation can be much more useful than mountains of words' (p. 30). A combination of both methods is advocated because lectures alone give no training in self-development, and process-experiencing methods alone do not provide a clear enough theoretical insight. Consequently a subject may well be introduced in the form of a lecture but needs to be followed up by activities, discussions, workshops or other exercises which will give the participants the opportunity for an understanding of the subject by experiencing the process themselves. This combination of the two approaches might apply when dealing with topics such as communication, group dynamics, decision-making or the conduct of meetings.

A second example of learning through experience as an appropriate method for learning skills was given by Rosa Maria Gonzalez-Tirados in her paper to the Windsor workshop, describing a programme for the training of school directors being carried out at Madrid's Polytechnic University. The first module of this training, entitled 'The psychology of directors' deals with the following topics, which are worked on in groups:

1. Problem-solving in organizations.
2. Styles of leadership.

3. Motivation.
4. Group decision-making.
5. Inter-personal perception.

In designing the module use was made of David A. Kolb's model of learning through experiences.

> Each topic begins with the description of a concrete experience by a participant which means that the learning process is initiated not by traditional methods such as books, teachers or a classroom but through the participant's own particular 'lived experience'. Analysis and discussion of this experience then follow, so as to get a thorough assimilation and conceptualization which will lead to conclusions and generalizations likely to be applied to new experience. (Kolb *et al.*, 1971).

It is hoped that through this process of learning which begins with 'lived experience', directors may discover their own learning styles and their own approach to problem-solving in their schools. It is also claimed that this method gives directors a better understanding of leadership, of the complexities of working in groups and of leading groups.

It is evident from meetings with participants, course providers and trainers in a variety of European countries that the problem which most often exercises them in the area of methodology is how the inter-personal skills of management are to be taught effectively, e.g. inter-personal relationships, decision-making, negotiation, mediation, running meetings, handling and resolving conflict, leadership. There is a growing acceptance that such skills can only be learned effectively if an opportunity is provided for the learner to exercise the skill in question and be given feed-back on his or her performance. There is an area of debate between those who believe that such an experience can be provided in an artificial form such as role play or simulation and those who believe that such skills can only be effectively learned within the 'real' situation in which the learner is called upon to exercise them, namely in the school. This problem is unlikely to be resolved until there is a great deal more research evidence available.

Meanwhile, there does appear to be a general recognition that trainers faviour the deliberate inclusion of a wide variety of methods within any one training programme. The handbook produced in Norway and referred to above expresses it thus:

> Variation and change of method usually improve the effectiveness and the level of learning. As experience shows, some participants seem to benefit from one way of working, while others prefer a different way. (Seljelid, 1982, p.28).

The following methods of working are commonly in use in many countries and are summarized in the Norwegian handbook:

1. Lectures giving information and lectures giving inspiration.
2. Plenary sessions, discussions and questions.
3. Group work: task-oriented problem-solving exercises.
4. Group discussion: process-oriented discussion of questions arising in the group from case studies, 'real' or imaginary.
5. Role-play: situational role-play and simulation in group or plenary sessions; activities which lead to experiencing different types of behaviour.
6. Video recordings of group activities used as a basis for discussion of behaviour, etc. (p.28).

This list provides opportunities for both the cognitive approach in the lecture followed by plenary discussion and also for process-experiencing methods in group activities and role-play. It should be remembered that in addition to this course activity in Norway there is a second part of each course which takes place in the school, in which it is claimed that skills are exercised in the 'real' situation. A similar process is followed in Sweden. What seems uncertain so far in both countries is whether there is transfer of learning from the course sessions to activities within the 'real' school setting, and research evidence of this will be awaited with interest.

The above methods will not be examined in detail but there are a number of points to be made about their appropriateness in programmes for training school leaders.

Lectures and plenary sessions

Lectures represent a time-honoured method of teaching adults and clearly have a place in the teaching and learning of school leaders. However, education is their stock-in-trade and consequently they will usually be critical as well as appreciative of the performance of lecturers. It is of great importance, therefore, that lectures set a high standard of content and of quality in presentation. This is particularly true of the opening lecture in a training programme because it will set the tone for the course and help to condition the attitudes of the participants. Such an opening lecture in its standard of intellectual content, quality of presentation and professional relevance must establish credibility and arouse the hope that what is to follow will have something positive and valuable to offer. The lecture is also valuable as a relatively non-threatening teaching method which allows participants to learn anonymously. However, lectures may induce an attitude of passivity or of detachment unless they are sufficiently stimulating and provocative to capture the interest and involvement of the listeners.

Sister O'Shea makes a number of valuable points about the choice of lecturers for training programmes in Northern Ireland.

1. The lecturer should have credibility, arising from real knowledge and experience of running a school.
2. He should be aware of recent developments and current educational issues as they are affecting schools.
3. He should be conscious of how schools can differ and should encourage an awareness that there are no easy solutions applicable to all schools.
4. He should be capable of showing that different perspectives are possible on any educational question and that different interpretations of situations can lead to different decisions.
5. His presentation should be sufficiently general to range over the possibilities that can arise in different schools and thus help participants to broaden their perspectives beyond the narrow confines of their own institutions.

6. He should be able to do this in a cogent and lively manner, using not only all his personal resources but also any media resources which can enhance his presentation. (O'Shea, 1983)

Plenary sessions following lectures do not appear to be highly regarded by participants and the larger the audience the less valuable they are thought to be other than for seeking further clarification, explanation or elaboration of what has been said in the lecture. Likewise, plenary discussions are not a particularly popular opportunity for learning, as only a limited number of speakers can take part and some participants, although they may have valuable contributions to make, may be too nervous, anxious or shy to intervene. Again a participant from Northern Ireland may be quoted: 'Plenary sessions are like staff meetings—they should be short and held only when necessary'. (ibid.)

Group discussions

In all the training programmes surveyed in this study, group discussion is a method which plays a significant part. The method is extensively used throughout Europe and is valued greatly by participants and course organizers alike. In a small group members have the opportunity to air their views and share their experiences and their practices in a less threatening atmosphere. Group size is important and the optimum size appears to be no fewer than five and not more than ten members, the most commonly favoured size being seven or eight members. Such groups develop their own 'climate', ethos or atmosphere and can produce a cohesiveness which often lasts long after the training period is over. It is the writer's experience that discussion groups form a most potent learning environment for heads and senior staff, who because of their frequent professional isolation often lack precisely this close relationship with professional colleagues which builds up during the period of the training programme and enables them to gain confidence in sharing their insecurities, their anxieties and their problems in an atmosphere which is supportive and helpful. Many of the relationships established during the training persist long after the training period and lead to renewed meetings, reunions or visits to each other's schools. It will be suggested later that when seeking for methods of providing support and follow-up to a formal training programme it may be appropriate to bring together such groups at convenient intervals, because of the valuable mutual support which they provide.

While participants appear to appreciate remaining in one group for most of a training period there is some evidence that they also value the opportunity to be a member of other groups in order that they may encounter ideas in different contexts and share in a wider range of experience. The composition of groups is also important and it is well worth devoting time and care to this task. It may be a deliberate policy, as it was at the Centre where the writer worked in England, to compose groups in such a way as to bring together a wide range of experience of different types of schools, namely, urban and rural, large and small, selective and non-selective, single-sex and co-educational. However, at particular times during a course it was found appropriate to compose more homogeneous groups such as heads, deputy heads and advisers or inspectors who met separately to discuss matters of mutual interest or anxiety.

Group leadership is everywhere recognized as being of crucial importance and the selection and training of people to fulfil this demanding role is dealt with later. Particular skills are necessary for the successful leading of group discussion and the word 'leader' is used deliberately because a 'neutral' chairman is not, in general, favoured. Nor is a very dominant or directive style of leadership appropriate, as this merely inhibits discussions and frustrates those with contributions to make. Feedback in the evaluation of training in Northern Ireland suggests that it is important for group leaders to be consistent and predictable, giving a sense that they are in control. On the issue of too much or too little direction, principals felt that a discussion which was too tightly structured did not allow group members to introduce issues which were significant to them, while if the group was allowed to range freely over any number of issues they were equally disappointed.

139

Group leadership is, of course, a study in itself but suffice it to say that group leaders need highly developed skills in human interaction, notably a sensitivity to group atmosphere, an understanding of the mental and social processes going on the group, and an ability to draw out the shy and reluctant participant while dealing diplomatically or even sometimes firmly with the member who seeks to dominate, or simply talks too much. Heads and senior staff of schools are used to exercising authority and often themselves are chairmen of committees. Consequently, when brought together into in formal discussion groups they may not always be the easiest of folk to manage.

Role play and simulation exercises

There is evidence that role play is a training method which is widely used in programmes in which social processes and personal awareness are being explored. It is not proposed to examine its justification on psychological or sociological grounds but to report briefly the reactions of heads and the impressions gathered by the writer from his own involvement with training programmes. Role play appears to be a method of learning of which heads are sceptical unless the exercises involving this method have been carefully structured and unless the scenarios have been composed with the maximum attention to realism. When the roles of the participants have been portrayed with skill and insight into attitudes and human behaviour there may be a lively response and a learning situation may well develop. However, if the material provided does not demonstrate that the trainers are closely in touch with the day-to-day problems of running schools then the results will seldom be satisfactory and the exercise may well invite ridicule.

Much the same may be said of the reactions of participants to simulation exercises. We have already encountered the arguments for using simulation as compared with reality as a basis for learning. Simulations often figure in training programmes and it is a personal view that they can be successful when they are prepared with the greatest care and in the fullest detail. A great deal of information may need to be provided using a variety of media. An exercise of this nature might require a small production team of, say, three or four persons including individuals with writing and dramatic skills and technical expertise. The materials produced might include video-taped sequences, slide and tape sequences and role plays as well as considerable background material and documentation. All this might take some six months to produce and demand creativity and imagination combined with a firm grip on reality. There is no doubt that such exercises can engage the interest and enthusiastic involvement of heads and they are prepared to devote time and energy to working on them once they are convinced of their professional relevance and their credibility.

Clive Hopes made a strong plea for trainers to diversify the inner structure of their training schemes in his paper presented to the Gatwick conference. He maintains that the emphasis is too often on the 'comfortableness' of working papers, lectures, handouts and group work, methods which encourage a rather passive approach on the part of participants. Furthermore, the adoption of more challenging methods is seen as a threat to both trainers and to participants.

> The development of in-basket exercises, simulations and role-playing situations is arduous and time-consuming; it demands far more creativity and activity than writing a paper in an 'ivory tower'. The participants, on the other hand, are confronted with difficult situations, in which their responses and behaviours are exposed and challenged by their colleagues on the course. It is not as comfortable as sitting in a circle wisely discussing issues. [See ATEE and NAHT, 1982].

In concluding the section on training methods, reference should also be made to the relationship of time to the effective learning of certain skills and attitudes. Hopes (1982) makes the point that, for example, human relations training can be better achieved by a series of events or experiences over a longer period of time.

Experienced group dynamics trainers know that the

principles cannot be effectively practised and internalised in a couple of days or compressed neatly into a one-week course. A careful examination of approaches to the study of group processes is necessary for their meaningful incorporation into training, rather than 'one shot' popular events.

The trainers

Following a comparatively brief look at 'how' school leaders may learn we turn to the second issue of methodology, namely, 'who' the appropriate teachers or trainers are. The first question to consider is who should direct the training programmes, and to this question two positive answers seem to be emerging in the European programmes. The first is that it is highly desirable, if not essential, that the directors of teams of trainers should hold full-time appointments. In those countries where national schemes are established, the directors are all able to give their full attention to this work. It is the writer's experience that when the training of senior school staff is given over to advisers, inspectors or those who may have already a heavy burden of responsibility for other areas of the education service, they are unable, with the best will in the world, to carry out the training to the high standards of preparation or presentation that have been advocated above. In Sweden, the post of team leader in each region is a full-time appointment, usually a seconded head; in France, the *inspecteur d'académie* responsible in each area has increasingly found that the training has become a full-time task; in the Netherlands the national centre has a full-time staff. At the regional centre where the writer worked there was a full-time directorate of three. The second answer concerns the crucial issue of credibility and that suggests that those who direct training programmes should have had experience of running schools. This is a strongly held view of many participants from different countries. It would appear that heads and senior staff place a heavy emphasis on the need for those responsible for their training to have a thorough knowledge and understanding of the real problems which face those running schools today. They also claim to be able to learn a great deal from their colleagues or former colleagues and to respect highly those who have acknowledged experience as heads of what are generally reputed to be or to have been 'good' schools.

There is a wider variation of view as to who the other tutors or trainers should be, but again there is a strong body of opinion that heads themselves and practitioners have an important role to play in the training of their colleagues. At the Gatwick conference there was considerable support for the idea that teams of trainers should include heads and other practitioners as well as trainers from higher education and others.

> For course provision to be effective, those running the courses should have credibility with their students. The input from practitioners is of vital importance, especially at the 'information' stage. [ATEE and NAHT, 1982].

The same conference recognized that no individuals or groups had a monopoly of wisdom and teams might well include, in addition to experienced practitioners, advisers, inspectors, university and college lecturers and contributors from business and industry. A number of participants in the Gatwick conference from different European countries illustrated how training teams were composed. Helt reported that in France training teams are chosen from the 'best professionals', who have skills in adult education. These include headteachers, deputies, some teachers, bursars, administrators from education authorities, school doctors and social assistants. However, headteachers form the majority *(ibid.)*. Van Daele reported that, in Belgium, heads were used to present topics to other members. He also stated that heads who have completed the training were used as trainers but said that there was a problem in finding teachers with a knowledge of personnel management who also knew schools well *(ibid.)*. Stegö explained that in Sweden the team includes headteachers, psychologists, inspectors and advisers and that there was great benefit in having a mixture of experience and specialisms in the training team: 'Heads ask why there are so many psychologists in the training teams and it is important to remind them that people are drawn out of the specialisms to become members of the training team' *(ibid.)*.

It is interesting to note that when lists of potential members of training teams were given to the writer by participants, heads and 'practitioners' were always mentioned first and undoubtedly they rank highly as a source of both expertise and support. However, Hopes qualifies their role as trainers thus:

> A successful principal may not necessarily be very analytical about describing the reasons for his success. One must be wary of the assumption that such persons are the best for developing the training assignment. In some cases, the most useful principals to have are those who have had training themselves and have had the opportunity to order the ideas gained from their experience into a conceptual framework provided by theory, but moderated by actual practice. *(Ibid.)*.

Certainly, this writer would endorse the importance of the role to be played by practising heads in training programmes as lecturers and particularly as course tutors and leaders of group discussions. As has been explained earlier, the part played by practising heads as consultant course tutors at the North West Educational Management Centre in England cannot be overestimated. Their contribution to both the planning of programmes and to their implementation, as well as to the building up of a body of expertise in the region has been outstanding. Having made that statement, however, it must also be said that good consultant tutors are not all that easy to identify. There is a limited pool of expertise in this field and choice of trainers depends as much on personality as on status. They must have credibility with their colleagues as well as with their employers. The latter will not readily release them for the work unless they are confident that schools will not suffer by their absence, however temporary.

Training the trainers

It is now becoming generally recognized that trainers need training. This poses problems at a time when resources do not

144

always permit the provision of the necessary basic training for school leaders. Hopes again makes the pertinent comment that:

> 'Training the trainers' is an important pre-condition for the effective expansion of schemes for the professional development of principals. The term means more than passing on 'know-how' for certain techniques in running courses. It refers to the need to train trainers to analyse the objectives, to practise appropriate methods for their achievement and to develop relevant materials. [ATEE and NAHT, 1982].

Perhaps the most important area in which the training of the trainers is necessary is that of inter-personal relationships, particularly those skills necessary in handling groups.

The national training programmes in Sweden and in France have built-in training at regular intervals for the members of their training teams and these have been described in the case studies drawn from those countries. In both these countries the trainers are brought together centrally and so have the added advantages of meeting trainer colleagues who are working in other areas of their countries, as well as receiving stimulus from the central co-ordinating agency. However, in less centralized systems, a regional team, if it includes a broad range of experience, can undertake its own 'in-house' training. Members of a team can thus improve their own training skills and also develop training materials in workshop sessions.

In France the Commission chaired by de Peretti envisages four categories of trainers for such programmes in the future:

1. Experts who would be university or profession-based and who would be responsible for lifting the level of theoretical and conceptual input. They would enlarge the frames of reference and enrich the experience of participants.
2. Practitioners who would bring particular competences or experience.
3. *Animateurs* who would have skills in methodology and who would be permanent members of a team but for a limited period, returning to their jobs after a time. They

would be responsible for method and for evaluation and would be general 'facilitators' of training.

4. Others, such as parents, pupils and employers, who would make contributions from the environment outside schools to provide the perspectives of the clients.

Practitioners might be given a short period of training and *animateurs* might require a longer and broader training (Peretti, 1982, pp. 193-4).

Consultants

A final word is necessary in this chapter on the role of consultants in the training of heads and senior staff. Consultants play a significant part in those training programmes which are concerned to go beyond the development of the individual head or deputy head to the development of a school where the head is seen as a change agent, and the consultant provides an additional resource to help bring about change in a school. It must be said that little research evidence is available yet to reveal in what circumstances a consultant is necessary or what makes a good consultant. Nevertheless, consultants in the above sense are taking part in both the Swedish and the Norwegian training programmes.

Stegö reported at Gatwick that trainers in Sweden visit the participants in their own schools five times over the two-year period of the course. 'It is this regular local contact over an extended period of time that is intended to prepare school leaders and their schools for change' (ATEE and NAHT, 1982). There are clearly problems in making more frequent visits in a country in which schools are widely dispersed, and participants and trainers in Sweden voiced some concern over the effectiveness of these visits in helping to bring about change. Perhaps a closer working relationship between school and consultant is necessary over a longer period.

Per Kvist gave an account of the work of the consultant in Norway, an account which is further developed in his paper *Leadership in Schools: A Norwegian Programme for Improvement* (Kvist, 1982c), which is published by the Sheffield City Polytechnic in England as one of the Sheffield papers in educational management. These papers describe the programme carried out in the Hordaland region of Norway. Consultants are an integral part of this programme and are recruited from teachers, school psychologists, or from the staff of the two teacher training colleges in the County of Hordaland. They partake in the leadership training prgramme as part of their training which begins some six months before the course for school leaders starts. They are recruited in pairs (often a teacher and a psychologist) to work as a team. They are relieved of one to two hours of the normal job in order to compensate for working in one or two schools and in one study group. Their task is to facilitate planned organizational change through group work with staff at a school. Consultants, with the staff, undertake an analysis of the situation of the school using a diagnostic instrument of 40–50 items. The teachers then decide what they want to tackle as priorities. The results of the enquiry are then analysed by the planning group, i.e., the head and two elected teachers. The role of the consultants thereafter is to meet the needs of the school in undertaking the development process and to help as and when they are required.

In the national programme at present being developed in Norway, provision is made for consultants but they are not an integral part of that programme. If a school requires the services of a consultant it will make the necessary arrangements. Directors of Education in counties may facilitate this process by providing lists of available consultants and by arranging consultant training courses. One problem identified in Norway is the shortage of suitable people to act as consultants. The Norwegian handbook referred to earlier states:

> It is not always easy to find such people. Although the training of consultants is taking place in various regions at the moment, it seems unlikely that the need for good consultants will be fully met for some time. [Seljelid, 1982, p.36].

Per Kvist in his Sheffield paper provides the content of his training course for consultants. It includes organization theory, climate, communication, problem-solving, conflict resolution, leadership and, of course, the role of the consultant.

The role of the consultant is clearly complex. It implies a dynamic and developing relationship with the school and its staff, which usually begins with the school initiating the consultancy and inviting in the consultant who in turn then needs to 'negotiate the entry' to the school. Only the clients can decide what is useful for them, and the consultant at this stage is establishing relationships and preparing for the next stage as facilitator or catalyst. The relationship established may be temporary and specific to an immediate problem or development, or may become more permanent. It is the experience of the writer that it is often difficult to break away from a consultancy relationship once established or to 'extricate' oneself from the school. It is often necessary to negotiate a 'contract' with the school regarding what is to be attempted and what time allocation the consultant is able to devote to this role. A consultant is usually in an advisory role and does not provide or prescribe solutions. It is therefore important that he or she does not stand in a hierarchical position in relationship to the school staff. This means that local education advisers or inspectors may find difficulty in working in this way. There is some research evidence for this from Bolam, Smith and Canter (1978). Likewise, credibility is very important and consequently college staff also find the consultant role difficult in schools because they often lack credibility in the eyes of teachers and heads. They have to break down prejudice and cut through the stereotypes,.in order to demonstrate clearly their expertise and their capacity to provide practical help.

The most difficult type of consultancy to provide for a school involves processes such as decision-making, communication and problem-solving procedures. All of these processes involve inter-personal relationships and the consultant may have to deal with power and authority and how it is exercised by people in the school. Very personal issues such as leadership style may have to be faced, which can be very threatening to those concerned unless a very 'open' atmosphere has been created. Such a process can take a long time.

The consultant performs the role of objective external observer without any vested interest in outcomes. In contrast to the traditional trainer he is often required to be a specialist in diagnosing and identifying needs. He may then need to concentrate on the problem-solving process, presenting a number of options but without prescription. He may influence the eventual decisions but should rarely prejudice issues, dismiss alternatives or press too vigorously particular viewpoints. This role is very difficult and requires skills of listening followed by an ability to build up an atmosphere of openness and trust among the members of staff concerned while recognizing that confidentiality needs to be respected throughout the process.

Valuable information on the role of the consultant is being gathered from a Schools Council project in England known as GRIDS (Guidelines for Review and Institutional Development in Schools). A number of useful handbooks have been produced to accompany the project which is based in the University of Bristol Department of Education under the leadership of Ray Bolam, and one of these (first draft 1982) is entitled 'Guidelines for staff and external consultants working in GRIDS project schools'. The handbook distinguishes two types of consultancy which may be valuable. One is concerned with the 'process' of managing the review, gaining staff involvement and decision-making. Reference has already been made to this role. The other responds to a need for 'expert' consultancy from a specialist in a particular field which is relevant to the review or development in an individual school. One person may act as both 'process' and 'expert' consultant but sometimes it will be appropriate for the staff to work with two or more people. A series of general principles is offered which should be observed when a consultant is brought into a school.

1. Information about the school that an external consultant acquires should be regarded as strictly confidential;
2. the external consultant should, as a matter of courtesy, not visit the school without informing the head;
3. the external consultant must be prepared to make a fairly long commitment to the school if this is required;
4. the external consultant should be prepared to work collaboratively with the staff;
5. the external consultant should endeavour to act as a facilitator and not be either prescriptive, i.e., telling the

staff what to do, or judgmental, i.e., telling the staff that particular things are right or wrong;

6. the staff should be as clear and specific as possible about their requests when they invite an external consultant to help them;

7. the staff should be realistic in their expectations of the external consultant, e.g. about the time he or she can spend in the school;

8. the staff should be prepared to work collaboratively with the external consultant and should be prepared to be flexible when necessary;

9. some form of 'contract' clarifying the agreement between the staff and the external consultant is desirable and it may be helpful to write this down.

The handbook also offers a useful checklist to schools of the tasks and stages of acquiring, introducing and involving an external consultant in a school review and a subsequent plan of action for development (*ibid.*, pp. 1–6).

A head whose school was participating in the project added further useful comments based upon his experience (Davies 1983). The relationship which the consultant establishes with a school might involve:

- skills in the role of 'listener';
- flexibility in responding to perceived needs;
- providing encouragement at times and at others being the target or 'sponge' for the feelings and frustrations of others over contentious issues;
- powers of reasoning, persuasion and empathy, in helping others to define or redefine their goals and values;
- being perceived as non-threatening to all by a lack of executive power, yet powerful in terms of the exercise of the above skills.

Davies also stressed that a school should be allowed to appoint a consultant of its own choice and to negotiate with the consultant the *modus operandi* and boundaries of the role. In seeking a suitable consultant a school would need to consider whether he or she has:

- the relevant experience;
- sufficient professional standing;
- a sympathetic attitude to the style of the school and the process to be undertaken;
- the time agreed as required for the process;
- the relevant skills and expertise.

He also makes the final point that 'the major activity of the consultant will be relating to people, making personal qualities, inter-personal skills and general awareness the more relevant requirements' (p.12).

Much still remains to be learned about the role of consultants working in the school situation. The relationship between the external consultant and the school is a sensitive one and the internal team of teachers plays an equally crucial role in establishing that relationship and following through any development in the school. Local education authorities may also play a part by developing expertise in the change process involving consultants, teachers and administrators. Further evidence will be awaited with interest from the research which is taking place in Norway and in Sweden and from such projects as that briefly described above which is taking place in England. Doubtless, evidence will be emerging also from other European countries where the role of the consultant is being developed. Meanwhile, both Fullan (1982) and Schmuck (1981) are valuable sources on the development of the consultant's role in American and Canadian schools.

If, as is the case in certain countries already, the training of school leaders is seen to involve not only a training programme outside the school but also the provision of support and help for school leaders in bringing about change and development in their schools, then the role of the external consultant may become a very significant one in the training process. The education services in those countries which adopt this process are developing a new form of educational professional. Such individuals require qualities and expertise which have not been those most frequently needed by educationists. They are not the qualities or expertise expected of the average teacher, adviser, lecturer or administrator. Consequently, when such people have been identified, and if they can be identified in sufficient numbers, then an appropriate training will have to be provided for them if they are to perform effectively what is clearly a most demanding and responsible job.

CHAPTER 5

Some Issues of Evaluation

Evaluation of training programmes in school management is one of the major problems facing the providers of such programmes. During a period when financial restraints inhibit the development of all forms of in-service training in the field of education, it seems even less likely that resources will be made available for independent evaluation programmes. Providers and trainers are thus faced with the dilemma of urgently needing to justify the efficacy of their activities to those who provide them with financial support, and yet are unable to seek the very evidence which might establish that justification. What was evident at the Windsor workshop was the relative lack of research in the field of school management training, the great need for such research in all the countries represented and also the complexity of the task. In the final report Hegarty refers to the limited achievements so far in this area.

> On the face of it, we know very little from research about school leadership training and its effectiveness. Throughout the week we have heard how little research there has been conducted, as delegates described the limited state of practice in their own countries. Certainly, if we take a strict definition and confine ourselves to studies explicitly about school leadership training, there is little to report apart from the studies of the Swedish school leader education programme. (Hegarty, 1982).

He adds later that:

> Very little progress has been made on measuring the effectiveness of school leadership training programmes.

153

This should occasion regret but not dismay. Quite simply, the task is singularly difficult. Given the range and complexity of the variables involved and the limited resources available for evaluation, it is only to be expected that limited progress will have been made.

'Effectiveness' is a word frequently met when the issue of evaluation is being discussed and criteria for evaluation are being sought. The elusive nature of the term illustrates the difficulty inherent in evaluating in-service training programmes. In asking whether a training programme for school leaders has been 'effective', we may be asking questions about the persons who have been trained or about their schools. Have the persons changed in terms of knowledge, skills or attitudes? Is their behaviour different, or as total personalities have they changed? Alternatively or in addition, have the schools changed in any way, have changes taken place in organization, in the attitudes and behaviour of the teaching staff or in the learning experiences of the children? In attempting to examine or analyse the 'effect' on an individual or on an institution which may have been brought about by a programme of training, one is faced with the intractable problem of distinguishing those changes which may have been brought about by the training from those which may be attributable to other sources or influences. Some changes may have been brought about by a complex mixture of influences and again others may be short-lived and be followed by reversion to former practices.

Changes in group attitudes or behaviour, in organization or in whole institutions, are perhaps the most difficult to evaluate. Once one attempts to go beyond the measurement of pupil outcomes expressed in terms of academic achievement or examination success to examine such aspects as social development, the professional development of staff, job satisfaction, or school ethos and atmosphere, the task becomes very difficult, although not impossible, as is evident from the study by Rutter *et al.,* (1979) *Fifteen Thousand Hours.* Any attempt to associate these aspects of school development with a specific training programme undertaken by an individual head is a very different matter. To quote Hegarty again:

The distance between school leadership training and institutional outcomes is so great and so indirect that the problems of practical measurement assume a new order of difficulty and on occasion seem virtually insoluble. (1982).

Glatter instances a further and associated dimension of difficulty:

Testing the claims for effectiveness of group development clearly raises acute methodological problems. In particular, examining whether intended changes actually occur is a major research task. (Glatter, 1983).

In his view the process of change in schools is still 'very incompletely understood' and he quotes the work of Bolam (1981) who, when investigating innovation in schools, suggests that it is a highly complex process and the result of many organizational pressures and constraints:

Such changes, it is argued, are frequently small scale, incremental, and multi-faceted . . . Most schools are dealing simultaneously with several changes and innovations which vary in size, complexity and urgency.

Per Kvist reporting to the Gatwick Conference on the evaluation programme in Norway (Hordaland) where 'the head is seen as a change agent' stresses the complexity of the task of assessing change in a school, even in the form of 'impression':

It is a very complex task to undertake follow-up of this kind and to get the 'feeling of change'. Results seem to vary —some schools report more problems than before (or perhaps an awareness of these problems). Time is needed for schools to adapt. (ATEE and NAHT, 1982).

Not only does very little research evidence exist, but it would appear to be quite difficult to persuade researchers to undertake such work. The writer's personal experience at the North West Educational Management Centre was that repeated attempts to have the work of the Centre evaluated by independent researchers met with considerable reluctance on their part until the study by Hughes was published in 1981.

However, in spite of the difficulties which have been illustrated and the lack of what may be formally described as research, it is not to say that there is little evaluation of school-leader training programmes in Europe; in fact, there is a great deal. Most training programmes with which the writer is acquainted have been evaluated in a traditional fashion whereby participants and often trainers have been asked in a questionnaire or in discussion to comment upon the course content as well as on such matters as domestic arrangements, the value of group discussions or the personal benefits derived from the course. Such evaluations, while they cannot be classified as research, nevertheless are of considerable value to course providers in giving them instant feed back at the conclusion of (or sometimes even during) a course. Such information enabled adjustments and modifications to take place in course arrangements, and provides tutors, lecturers and course directors with perspectives on their own performances. However, such questionnaires or discussions have their limitations. They are often completed under the influence of 'post-course euphoria' and may simply tell the course directors what they want to hear. Clive Hopes (1982) in his paper 'Research and evaluation attempts in the Federal Republic of Germany' given to the Windsor workshop outlines some of the problems of this method of evaluation:

> The criticism of these forms is that they are usually 'measures of satisfaction'. They do not measure a person's acquisition of new knowledge or skills, nor do they guarantee implementation of new ideas, or changes of behaviour, even though good marks have been given. (Hegarty (Ed) 1982).

Hopes also makes the point that while a particular course session may have been rejected through poor presentation, it may equally have been rejected through lack of awareness or realization on the part of some participants of its significance as valued by others. Likewise, other participants may have found certain material too challenging or threatening. Nevertheless, this type of evaluation remains for many course providers the only measures of their success or failure.

In spite of the difficulties which have been illustrated and the consequent lack of substantial research material arising from training programmes for school leaders, some research *has* taken place and it is appropriate to give some details of major evaluation programmes which have taken place in Europe, or are taking place at the time of writing.

Sweden

The Windsor workshop recognized that more research had taken place into school leader training in Sweden than in any other country and Mats Ekholm, one of the directors of the national programme which is co-ordinated from the University of Linköping, presented a paper to the workshop which outlined the extent of this research work in Sweden. (In: Hegarty, 1982). Ekholm instanced some 38 reports on the school leader training programmes in Sweden, which cover a wide variety of topics such as the history of the programme, its basic philosophy and ambitions, formal and informal arrangements, the training methods, the conditions of working and the traces left by the training. Three pieces of work are of particular interest in relation to the aims of the programme which, as we have already seen, is concerned with the development of the individual school leader as a change agent and consequently with the development of the school. A major study was carried out by Glenn Hultman of the University of Linköping under the title: 'Organisational development through management training' which was published in 1981. This study is particularly relevant to the points made earlier in this chapter about the difficulties of evaluating change in schools. Hultman studied the first two generations of participants in the training programme, those of 1976–77 and of 1977–78. Data were obtained by means of a study of documentary material prepared for the training and by a detailed questionnaire completed by 506 of the possible 670 participants. In the investigation a distinction was made between a programme focusing on the individual and one focusing on the organization. The questionnaire showed that the training had not been carried out entirely according to the aims of the trainers. This led Hultman to the conclusion that the training had been focusing on the individual and therefore would influence the school leader and his role but would be less likely to influence the development of the school.

The questionnaire was built up by the use of a number of questions which would indicate changes which had occurred. For example, the following question was intended to measure the effects of the programme on the participant's personal development: 'In what ways have you been influenced by the training?' An analysis of the responses to this question is given in Table 3.

Table 3

	1976/7 %	1979 %
1. I have to a certain degree changed my attitude towards people and things.	24	22
2. I have to some degree also changed my personal pattern of work and my personal behaviour.	41	47
3. My whole person has been involved in the change. Even my self-esteem has changed to some degree.	22	21
4. I have not changed.	11	9
(the question not answered).	2	1

N=506 N=548

(N=Number of respondents)

In the above table the first (1976/7) column is taken from Hultman's study and the second (1979) from a later generation of participants who were asked the same question by Ekholm. These latter responses were quoted by Eskil Stegö to the Gatwick Conference. Most participants in both the generations indicate that they have been influenced to some degree as persons and about one fifth say that their whole person has been changed.

Another question asked whether others had told them that they (the school leaders) had changed during the two years in which they had participated in the training. 22 per cent of participants said that this was so.

One of the questions that was used to measure in what ways the school leaders felt that their functioning had been influenced by the training was put in this way:

Q57. What concrete consequences did the training have on the way you allocate working time in the following areas?

The results (see Table 4) are again given for two generations.

Such results and others of the same kind have some obvious disadvantages because they are self-declarations and therefore are highly subjective and probably over-estimate change.

Table 4 Responses to Q57

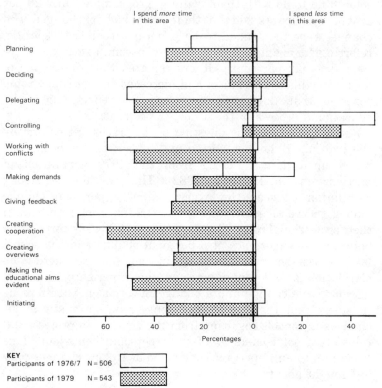

However, Ekholm, in a paper presented in Strasbourg in 1980 reviewing the evaluation of in-service education of teachers in Sweden, has made the valid comment that while such responses cannot be seen as measures of change, nevertheless they are of value in perceiving the 'message' which the participants have taken from the training. They also help us to understand the 'traces' that are left in the minds of those who have taken part in the training programme (pp. 13-14). The evidence suggests that there has been some norm-shifting among the school leaders in Sweden who have taken part in the training programme.

Other questions explored how the participants perceived the change and developmental process in their school. Most perceived some change and 'thought' that the change had something to do with their training programme. Only 26 per cent of participants said that their school had not changed. The changes reported tended to be general rather than specific, referring, for example, to the 'climate' becoming more 'open' to new ideas (22 per cent). Others reported that the degree of democracy inside the school had increased (16 per cent). Some reported that the programme had had effects upon the educational process in the school (8 per cent).

Pursuing further this question of the traces left behind by the training Ekholm reported at Windsor on his own work based upon data collected from the 1979 generation of participants (in Hegarty, 1982). This revealed a strong correlation between the experience of a personal change among the participants and their experience of a change in their professional roles. There is also a rather weak correlation between the experience of a personal change and the school leaders' assessments of a change in their schools. There is no correlation at all found between the experience of a pro-fessional role change and a change in a school. Therefore he considers that there are no reasons to be optimistic about changes in schools resulting from the changes in professional roles of school leaders or of their personal behaviour. This leads him to an important conclusion as to how changes may be brought about:

Changes in schools have to be directly implemented through

the training programme. There has to be direct action by the participants themselves if the objective of school development is to be attained. (Ibid.)

Ekholm sums up the overall picture of the Swedish training programme for school leaders, as revealed by research studies, by concluding that it is very positively received by participants but that

The weakest parts of the programme seem to be the linkages between what is learned during the course periods and what is done in the home periods. The results of evaluative studies show that the programme can be quite successful in influencing personal development, professional role development and school development. However, the results also indicate that there are no easy connections between the development of the school and the other kinds of development. There seems to be a need for more direct action on school development in the programme if it is to be successful in achieving the third major objective. (Ibid.).

The third example of research taken from Sweden has not yet been completed but reference must be made to it because of its importance in relation to the long-term effects of training. The model for this piece of research is based on the assumption that development in a school is a slow process. Hence, it is not possible to see the effects of an innovation until at least five years have passed (Ekholm, 1979). Therefore, the model adopts a five year period of evaluation. There is also a need to look at the whole school in order to understand what is happening.

About 36 schools which started the school leader training in 1980 have been invited to take part in this evaluation exercise. Two evaluators visited each school for about three or four days before the leaders entered the training period, their task being to obtain a clear picture of the state of the school. The instruments used by the evaluators were many group interviews, combined with individual interviews and also their own observations of the school. Before the visit, the head completed a questionnaire, giving some basic facts about the school; e.g., numbers of pupils and staff, whether any in-service activities were going on, and so on.

During the visit the evaluators tried to cover the following:

1. The aims of the school.
2. The organization of the school.
3. Patterns of work: methods, grading, planning, etc.
4. The decision-making processes: informal and formal processes, the involvement of staff and of pupils, etc.
5. Use of resources.
6. Any developments taking place.
7. Evaluation: routines for reporting and monitoring, etc.

After their first visit to the school the evaluators composed a report, locking it away afterwards. The same evaluators returned to the school in 1982. On this second visit they repeated the same procedure but added questions about the training programme which had taken place. At the conclusion of their visit a new report on the current situation was produced and locked away with the first report. The evaluation will be completed by a third and final visit to the school which should take place in 1985. During this visit the same procedures will be followed as on the two former occasions. As before, the evaluators will produce a report on the current situation but then they will attempt to judge what changes have taken place during the five years under review. This report will be presented to the staff of the school for discussion and for their approval. The final report will then be analysed together with the reports from other schools that have participated in the evaluation exercise.

The results of this research study in Sweden will be awaited with great interest for the light which, it is hoped, will be shed on long-term changes in schools and whether such developments can be attributed specifically to individual influences and to the training programmes in particular.

Northern Ireland

The second example of an evaluation report on a specific training programme is taken from Northern Ireland. A management education programme for principals and senior staff of post-primary schools was initiated by the Department of Education for Northern Ireland in 1980 and the Northern Ireland Council for Education Research was invited to undertake a formative evaluation of the programme. The evaluation extended over the first two years of the programme and a full-time research worker, Sister A. T. O'Shea, was appointed to carry out the exercise. Sister O'Shea's report, *Management in Secondary Education,* was published in 1983.

The evaluation exercise in Northern Ireland was an integral part of the programme from the start. The researcher was a member of the Steering Committee and was able to monitor its work. She prepared and analysed evaluation questionnaires which all participants completed at various stages in the programme, observed plenary and group sessions, attended all lectures and made follow-up visits to schools from which participants came. The aims of the research were:

1. to provide information for course providers which would inform future programme planning;
2. to identify weaknesses in existing provision;
3. to promote evaluation as a dimension of the programme by seeking to nurture a professional awareness among participants, particularly with regard to the interface between course precept and school practice;
4. to develop a methodology of self-evaluation and school evaluation.

The evaluation was conceived in two phases:

1. the evaluation of the organization, planning, structure and sequence of each study-conference, considering the issues of quality, format, content and style.
2. the gaining of a longer-term perspective of the value to participants of the programme after they had returned to their schools for a period of three or four months.

This evaluation makes an interesting comparison with the work which has taken place in Sweden because this programme has as its major aim the improvement of the quality of management in schools, through the development of the individual principals and senior staff during training which takes place away from their schools, usually in a residential situation. Although the Northern Ireland programme is not described in this study, it bears a strong resemblance in format to the programme described earlier which takes place at the North West Educational Management Centre in England and in fact that programme served as a model when the one in Northern Ireland was being designed.

Sister O'Shea suggests that at least two types of evaluation are necessary: 'summative' evaluation which determines the worth of a particular programme either immediately or some time after it is completed, and 'formative' evaluation which provides feedback to the organizers, while the programme is taking place, enabling them to be aware of how the programme is meeting the needs of participants and alerting them to deficiencies in the programme. Sister O'Shea also emphasizes the problem of 'effectiveness' which created difficulties for the second phase of her evaluation:

> Individuals have different capacities for perception and growth as well as different potentialities for change and development. Professional development cannot be measured quantitatively in terms of an input-output model. Moreover, participants bring to each conference different levels of professional experience, different needs, different philosophies as to how schools should be managed, different personal skills and intellectual abilities. (O'Shea, 1983, p. 13).

Any study of 'effectiveness' would, therefore, require the monitoring of 'effects' on the management of schools over an extended period. As the time scale of her own exercise was short

> The best that could be hoped for was to get from participants a post-conference perspective on the programme after a lapse of three to four months, to ask if any initiatives undertaken or planned had been stimulated by the management programmes and to enquire as to ways in which the conference programme had affected current operations. (p.13).

Nevertheless, principals were unanimous in their view that attendance at the conference had been a worthwhile experience, in making them more alert and aware of the importance of their role. It had provided new ideas and stimulated fresh thinking. However, an important conclusion reached by the evaluator was that

> There is little evidence in the evaluation data that [the participants'] attendance had helped them to improve their actual performance, in terms of 'know-how', the development of new skills, or plans for action after their return to work. (Ibid., p. 66).

Principals spoke of the difficulty of translating the theory of school management into practical activity. Learning 'that' may not necessarily be the best way of learning 'how'. The real worth of theory must surely lie in the degree to which it improves a person's practice or his knowledge of how to perform. Sister O'Shea makes the significant comment that

> Another way of looking at the participants' feelings of hesitancy with regard to their skills of implementation may be to acknowledge that a stage or further stages of management training of a more specific and practical nature may be required, if initial benefits gained in terms of understanding the scope and importance of the principal's role are not to be lost. (Ibid.).

As one principal put it, 'Perhaps there's another stage that we as principals will have to go through before we feel that we can take the initiative we want to take'. (Ibid.).

Sister O'Shea comes to the important conclusions that principals acquired a deeper knowledge and understanding of their role as managers from the conference and gained an overview of a wide range of management issues but the major deficiency in the programme was perceived to be at the level of skills development or 'know-how', i.e., interpersonal skills, curriculum development skills, implementation skills.

> Given, therefore, that the major aim of the management education programme was to improve the quality of management in schools, what can be said is that for many

principals the programme was the first step along the road to that goal but that it was clearly insufficient in itself. (Ibid., p.70).

Sister O'Shea devotes a final section of her report to the problems of bringing about change in schools and there is a close parallel between her conclusions and those of Mats Ekholm quoted earlier, namely that a major problem area is the linking of the course with the reality of the daily round in school. For principals there are constraints of returning to the everyday pressures of the school where, generally speaking, they are engaged in maintaining the system rather than in changing it. Above all, there is the major constraint of a requirement to change from the familiar role of maintenance to an unclear role of becoming active in curricular leadership in the school. As Fullan (1982) comments, 'It would appear from the data supplied by principals that they experienced considerable confusion and difficulty in trying to envisage what such a role change might entail'. (p. 72). It is significant that Ekholm's conclusions are very similar even though the training programme in Sweden has been in existence for a considerable time, has had school development as a specific aim and is a programme of much longer duration than that in Northern Ireland.

Detailed references have been made to the evaluation programmes in Sweden and in Northern Ireland because they seem to have practical implications for course providers, but that is not to say that other research in this field does not exist. Reference should also be made to two other pieces of work which are very relevant, one of which has been published and the other of which has still to be completed. In England M. G. Hughes published in 1981 a research report entitled 'Professional development provision for senior staff in schools and colleges'. While this study is not an evaluation of existing provision, it is valuable as a survey of the very large amount of training in educational management which has taken place in England and Wales. The report surveys both award-bearing and non-award-bearing courses and it undoubtedly influenced the decisions taken by the Department of Education and Science, and the subsequent initiative to step up the training of heads and senior staff, as is described in Chapter 3 of this study.

The other piece of research, which has yet to be completed, has already been referred to in the account given in Chapter 3 of developments in Norway. This is the research into the project 'The working milieu and school development' (AMS) in the Hordaland region of Norway. It was begun in 1981 by I. Njerve, J. Osnes and L. Vavik of the Stord College of Education. An interim report on this research was presented to the Windsor workshop and has been described earlier in this study. The work is due to be completed in 1984.

Clearly, we are only at the beginning of the process of evaluating training programmes for school leaders. On almost every topic mentioned in this study further research is needed to illuminate the way forward. A major task would seem to be that of devising methodologies for appraising changes in the personal development of heads and in the development of schools, and then identifying to what extent such changes can be attributed to the training which heads have received. However, there is unanimity that such training is necessary if heads and their colleagues are to be equipped to maintain schools in the present effectively and develop schools for the future. Provision of the appropriate training and accompanying research effort will require considerably more resources than are being made available at present. The readiness to provide such resources is a measure of a country's willingness to invest in the future of its young people.

CHAPTER 6

A Summary of Conclusions

In the final chapter of this study an attempt is made to draw some conclusions which may be useful to those who are working in the field. Inevitably such conclusions are personal and subjective but hopefully they may be of practical help to those who are contemplating setting up training programmes for the heads and senior staff of secondary schools or who may wish to review their existing provision in the light of recent developments in certain European countries.

The changing role of the secondary head

Significant changes are taking place in schools as they respond to the needs of a changing society and the changing needs of young people. The changes in schools are in the areas of curriculum, organization and leadership styles. Change creates a climate of anxiety and uncertainty in organizations and is affecting the role of the head of a secondary school in the following ways:

(a) The role is increasing in complexity and scope.
(b) The head is subject to increased pressures both from inside and outside the school.
(c) The head is subject to considerable personal stress which is brought about by an increased workload, by isolation and often by loneliness.
(d) Heads often have to devote more time to administrative tasks and have less time for educational tasks. This may be contrary to their wishes.
(e) The demands now being made on heads from many sources may often be conflicting and confusing.

(f) The job of the head is often 'a frantic succession of disconnected activities'.

(g) There is too little time for reflection and planning for the future.

(h) As long as change continues the role is an emergent rather than a stable one.

These conclusions represent firm impressions given to the writer but emphasis varies in different countries.

Some internal influences on the head

Changes in the head's role are taking place because of the increased part being played by teachers and pupils in the running of schools.

(a) Teachers are exerting pressures for more participation in the management of schools, in some cases supported by legislation.

(b) Teachers' unions and professional associations are more active in establishing and modifying conditions of service.

(c) Pressure groups among teachers are promoting particular curriculum matters.

(d) Teachers have representation on management committees of schools.

(e) Pupils are seeking participation in the running of schools and sometimes have representatives on management committees.

(f) Pupils are seeking opportunities to share in the negotiation of their learning programmes.

(g) Non-teaching staff play an increasing part in the day-to-day running of schools.

Some external influences on the head

A major change in the head's role is taking place as a result of the increased influences from outside the school. Consequently, there is a need for the head to devote more time and energy to external relationships with the following:

   (a) parents who are playing an increasing role in the running of schools

   (b) the members of management committees, governing bodies and local authorities who have become more influential

   (c) the members of the local community who have become increasingly involved in schools, e.g., politicians, employers, social workers

   (d) representatives of the press and of other media.

The influence of central government on schools varies greatly. There are examples of decentralization e.g., in France, Sweden, Norway and Denmark, and an example of increasing centralization in England.

The influences of different groups inside and outside secondary schools may vary and may contradict one another, thus leading to role conflict in ambiguity in the role of the head who has an increasing task of balancing and accommodating different demands and expectations. He also needs to communicate and interpret these demands from one group to another and often to negotiate, mediate and arbitrate between the different groups. The head has also become increasingly accountable to these different groups.

The 'present-future' dilemma

A major source of anxiety for the head of a secondary school is the need to manage the school in the present and at the same time to prepare the school for the future. In these conditions of considerable uncertainty a head needs to (a) maintain stability in the present and (b) act as a change agent for the future. These two aspects of the role may be in conflict because the activities of studying short-term and long-term futures and engaging (often with others) in the planning and implementing of change may disturb stability.

Leadership of a changing organization

The leader of a secondary school in these circumstances will increasingly need skills in managing people. The range of interpersonal skills required will be greater because:

(a) maintaining stability involves such skills as counselling, mediating, arbitrating and accommodating and
(b) a change agent also requires skills of goal-setting, gaining involvement and commitment, motivation and evaluation.

Leadership also requires certain qualities among which may be included drive, imagination, creativity, resourcefulness and a capacity to take risks. Vision and judgment are also necessary so that objectives are realistic and attainable. A head must give a school a sense of direction and a feeling of confidence.

The training needs of heads

There is a general consensus in the countries included in this study that in order to prepare the head of a secondary school to fulfil the exacting role described above, training is necessary. Furthermore, there is a growing recognition that such training should be a continuous process of development throughout the career of a head. There might be three possible stages in this professional development:

(a) initial training before or upon appointment,
(b) follow-up training in the first year or early years of experience as a head, and
(c) continuous training at regular intervals throughout the subsequent career of the head.

How are training needs identified?

Processes are needed to identify the training needs of heads in individual countries and in individual regions. Some methods which have been found successful are the following:

(a) Visits to course members before training programmes begin, to ascertain individual needs.
(b) Meetings of course members before training programmes begin, to discuss the needs of a group.
(c) Questionnaires, which are completed by course members at the end of training programmes.

(d) Visits paid to course members some time after the end of the training programme.
(e) Meetings with employing authorities who have nominated heads or senior staff for training.
(f) The appointment of practising heads as consultant course tutors who take part in the planning and organization as well as in the operation of training programmes.

Those methods which are retrospective do not benefit current course members but are valuable for evaluation purposes and for modifying future programmes.

The most difficult task is the individualizing of training needs to take account of past experiences, current skills and knowledge.

Frameworks of training needs

A variety of frameworks of training needs have been produced and a number have been referred to in this study. The most commonly mentioned 'areas' in which the training needs of heads are identified are the following:

(a) *Managing oneself,* e.g. self-awareness, self-development. Managing stress, managing time.
(b) *Managing people,* e.g. recruitment, sensitivity, staff development, communication, negotiation, mediation, arbitration, motivation, handling conflict, group behaviour, counselling.
(c) *Managing the curriculum,* e.g. curriculum appraisal, curriculum planning and development, monitoring classroom performance.
(d) *Managing organization,* e.g. setting up maintaining structures for consultation and decision-making, devising systems for record-keeping and documentation, delegating tasks and duties, routine management, establishing disciplinary procedures.
(e) *Managing change,* e.g. long-term strategy and planning, creative thinking, scenario building, goal-setting, implemeting change, responding to demands for change.

(f) *Managing external relations,* e.g. relating to national, regional or local systems, relating to parents, employers, politicians, the press and other media.

(g) *Leadership,* e.g. the contemporary role of the head in a changing school, leadership styles for organizational development.

(h) *Resources,* e.g. plant and equipment, financial management, budgetary control.

(i) *Law,* e.g. the law relating to schools and to young people.

Such frameworks are useful to the providers of training programmes as analyses of the range of knowledge and skills required to be an effective head. There is, however, increasing recognition that in devising a training programme great care is necessary in matching the topics to the specific needs of individuals and to the specific situations in which their schools are placed.

General conclusions concerning training needs

(a) The range of knowledge, skills and attitudes needed to be an effective secondary head is very wide and consequently the training needs are considerable.

(b) While some 'areas' of training may have figured in previous professional training, a substantial proportion of these 'areas' will not have been encountered before.

(c) Heads, on appointment, will have a wide variety of previous experience and background and consequently their training needs will vary considerably.

(d) Each of the 'areas' of need could be studied in varying degrees of depth.

(e) While there are a number of perspectives of need, e.g., those of the national or local educational systems, those of the trainers and those of the heads, it is important to give priority to those needs expressed by the heads themselves.

(f) While certain aspects of the 'areas' of need may be acquired by cognitive learning, e.g., resource management, finance and the law, a very considerable proportion of the skills involved, particularly those concerned with interpersonal relations, are most effectively learned in practical situations, by experience with feedback on performance.

(g) In view of the increasing pressures on the head from inside and outside the school, training needs may be closely related to the individual situation in which the school is placed.

(h) If training needs are closely related to the individual situation of a school, there is an argument for a substantial proportion of the training to be focused within the school.

The training of heads and senior staff of secondary schools

Organization

The development of training programmes for secondary heads appears to have taken place most rapidly in those countries where a national initiative accompanied by some national funding has led to the establishment of a central organizing body. These central bodies have usually produced national guidelines for the development of the training. In countries with comparatively small populations, e.g., Denmark, the Netherlands and Scotland the training has been effectively developed at one centre. In countries with larger populations e.g., France and Sweden, development has been rendered more effective by the establishment of a number of regional centres.

The role of central organizing bodies

The following are some of the tasks most commonly undertaken by centres which have been established nationally and where training takes place in regions.

(a) The drawing-up of national aims and guidelines for training.

(b) The training of trainers.

(c) The development of documentation and teaching materials.

(d) The establishment of a national bank of documentation and teaching materials.

(e) The identification of examples of good practice.
(f) The carrying-out of research programmes and the development of an underlying philosophy of training.
(g) The evaluation of regional training programmes.
(h) The co-ordination and circulation of the results of evaluation carried out in the regions.
(i) The national arrangements for funding the training programmes.
(j) The establishment of international links with other training programmes.

National centres are in most cases run by small full-time staffs including those with experience of running schools and those with an academic research background. There is usually a broadly based steering committee representing all interested parties.

National guidelines and frameworks

The following are examples of some of the areas in which national centres have issued aims and guidelines for the regional centres.

(a) Definition of the target population, e.g., whether training is for newly-appointed heads, for experienced heads, for heads and deputy heads.
(b) The duration of training programmes.
(c) Whether the training is to be full-time or part-time and the arrangements for the release of course members from their schools. These arrangements may include the provision of compensatory staffing for the school to cover for the head (or deputy head) during absence.
(d) Recommendations regarding time to be allocated by course members to matters related to their training, e.g., in Sweden four hours per week. This may also involve arrangements for providing compensatory staffing for the school.
(e) The arrangements for establishing and training regional training teams.
(f) Recommendations regarding the character of regional

training programmes, e.g., that they should develop a flexibility and a diversity of approach.

(g) Recommendations regarding the content and method of regional training programmes, for example:
  - emphasis on human relations training
  - contacts with employers, other professional organizations and social services
  - emphasis on practical as well as theoretical training
  - the inclusion of a residential element in the training programme
  - a period to be spent in an industrial or commercial concern.

(h) The production of a handbook for regional training teams with suggestions regarding the content and methods of training.

(i) Recommendations regarding appropriate follow-up training and continued in-service training for heads and deputy heads.

(j) Recommendations regarding the evaluation of the training by both staff and students.

Regional organization

Most regional centres have a small full-time directing staff with appropriate administrative support. In other respects there is considerable diversity and individuality in regional organization. Some centres have permanent premises for both administrative and training purposes. Others have administrative centres but carry out training programmes in separate premises such as colleges, conference centres, hotels or schools. Some are independent organizations while others are set within existing educational institutions. There are considerable advantages for regional centres to be as independent as possible of colleges or of local education authorities as this provides greater autonomy for trainers and creates a greater feeling of freedom, security and confidence among course members. The process of recruiting course members varies and methods include invitation, the acceptance of volunteers or nomination by the employing authority.

Regional centres are, in most cases, responsible for recruiting part-time trainers and exercise considerable autonomy and independence in the design and the carrying out of training programmes. Such centres build up their own ethos and traditions. Some have developed their own courses for the training of trainers while in other cases this is carried out at national level.

Types of training programmes

Three main types of training programmes are evolving in the countries which feature in this study. There are areas of overlap between these programmes but they may be distinguished as follows.

(a) Programmes of training which take the head or deputy head out of the school and provide training for him or her together with colleagues away from their schools. The aim is usually the training of the individuals to manage their schools more effectively. The main theme is the development of the individual. Examples: France and England.

(b) Programmes of training which are mainly concerned with the development of the school and with the role of the head as a change agent in that process. The training is focused mainly in the school and may involve other members of the school staff as well as the head and the deputy head. Example: Sweden.

(c) Programmes of training which combine the two former approaches, providing training for the head and deputy head as individual leaders and also aiming to develop the school as well. Examples: the Netherlands and Norway.

The first two programmes represent something of an ideological divide between an approach which originates in an in-service training tradition and an approach which originates in a tradition of organizational development.

The third type of programme may be seen as an attempt to reconcile the first two approaches.

Methods of training

Very little is known about the behaviour and motivation of heads or indeed of adults in a learning situation, or about the teaching methods which are most likely to be effective in their training. Consequently there is a wide range of teaching methods.

The duration of training

The duration of the training programmes varies greatly. There is a growing recognition that short training programmes for heads have a limited value beyond providing an awareness of the problems involved. Such courses, which last for one or two days or a week, are not effective in bringing about changes in the behaviour of people or in bringing about changes in schools.

(a) Training programmes which focus on individuals are now lasting a minimum of three weeks in England and three months in France.

(b) Training programmes which aim to initiate changes in schools last for a period of two years in Sweden.

(c) Training programmes which aim to train individuals as leaders and to initiate change in schools last for three years in Norway. There is gradual increase in awareness that major changes in schools, e.g., in curriculum, in organization or in decision-making processes, may take five or seven years. Changes must find a basis in the real needs of the whole school staff and solutions to problems must be experienced and become 'owned' by those who are to implement them. This process takes time.

(d) A further element which may add to the duration of training is a period spent in an industrial or commercial concern or in a department of the social services. The minimum period thought necessary for this experience to be valuable is two weeks.

Teaching methods in common use

(a) Lectures providing information and lectures providing inspiration.

(b) Plenary sessions, discussions and questions.
(c) Group discussions; process-orientated activities arising from the study of case-studies which may be imaginary situations or may be 'real' situations presented by individuals in the group.
(d) Workshop activities; task-oriented problem solving exercises designed for individuals or groups. The material may be imaginary or based on data brought from individuals' own schools.
(e) Role-plays or extended simulation exercises used for human relations training.
(f) Structured visits to institutions followed by plenary or group discussions.
(g) Video recordings of group activities used as a basis for discussion of behaviour.
(h) Individual projects leading to the presentation of an extended essay or of documentation in a variety of media.

Simulated or 'real' situations

A lively debate took place in Sweden between those who believe that the development of heads takes place more effectively in simulated situations and those who believe that training should take place in 'real' situations. This represents something of an ideological divide in methodology but the two approaches are not mutually exclusive and are combined in some training programmes.

Theory and practice

Many heads and senior staff of secondary schools are suspicious of theories and providers face a dilemma of how to introduce a conceptual basis into training programmes. There is a danger of training degenerating into the provision of 'practical tips' without a theoretical underpinning. It is advisable to move from practice to principle rather than the other way round.

General conclusions regarding particular methods

(a) Lectures need to be cogent, lively, stimulating and provocative and be followed by activities such as discussion in groups, exercises or 'workshops'. Alternatively, a topic for a lecture may be introduced by discussion of a case study. Plenary discussion is not very fruitful. Heads are a very critical audience and lectures need to be of a high quality in relevance, content and presentation. The credibility of lecturers is crucial.

(b) Group discussions provide a most valuable learning environment, much appreciated by heads and senior staff. Group size and composition is critical. Groups should have no fewer than five and not more than ten members: ideally seven or eight. The climate and ethos of groups is important, providing secure and close relationships with colleagues which is often lacking in their daily professional lives. A wide variety of experience within a group is valuable.

(c) Case-studies, simulations and role-playing: while the production of such material requires creativity and imagination, it needs to be firmly grounded in reality and should be scrutinized by practitioners before being used. Simulation exercises need to be prepared with care and attention to detail, possibly by a production team skilled in a variety of media, e.g., documentation, video tapes, film, slide-tape presentations, role-plays. Heads are somewhat sceptical of role-plays and the scenarios must, above all, be credible.

The trainers

(a) There is general acceptance that the posts of leaders of training teams should be full-time appointments. Advisers and inspectors have inadequate time to devote to this activity. Directors of training should have had successful experience as heads because credibility is vital.

(b) Opinions vary on the appropriate experience necessary to be a successful tutor. Practitioners have an important role to play but others such as advisers, inspectors, university and college lecturers and representatives from industry, commerce and the social services have a contribution to make, given that they can establish their credibility and have the necessary teaching skills.

(c) Consultant course tutors who are practising heads can play a very important role not only as discussion group leaders but as advisers on all aspects of training such as programme planning and the production of teaching materials. They keep full-time staff in touch with reality. Discussion group leaders play a very significant role and require sensitivity and human skills. They need to play a leadership role but not be dominant or directive. They should be consistent, flexible, predictable and remain 'in control'. Heads more readily accept other heads in this role than those from other professional backgrounds such as advisers, inspectors or college lecturers.

Training the trainers

Those who act as directors or as part-time consultant tutors and particularly those who are the leaders of discussion groups need development and training.

(a) They require opportunities for personal development, secondment, attendance at courses and visits both within their own countries and internationally if they are to broaden their outlook, develop wider perspectives and avoid the development of narrow, regional and local prejudices.

(b) Training of trainers may be carried out effectively at national or at regional levels and is particularly necessary in the field of interpersonal skills. Trainers also need to devote time to analysing and developing the aims and objectives of training programmes. They can share in the development of new teaching materials even when serving in a part-time capacity and have reported to the writer that meeting together with full-time directing staff to think through their ideas or to work through exercises is itself a most valuable form of staff development.

Consultants

There is an increasing recognition that consultants may have an important role to play in those training programmes which are concerned to initiate and implement change in schools. Difficulty may be experienced in recruiting a sufficient number of suitably qualified or appropriately experienced consultants to perform this role. Consultants need qualities and expertise not normally expected in other educational professionals such as teachers, advisers, inspectors or administrators.

Credibility is essential if they are going to negotiate 'entry' to a school and then negotiate a 'contract' with the school. They need to remain non-directive and non-judgmental particularly when dealing with situations involving power and authority. Their role may often be to act as facilitators or catalysts offering alternative options rather than prescribing solutions.

Consultancy is a complex role requiring training in a variety of human skills such as communication, group-dynamics, problem-solving and particularly the resolution of conflict. Consultants need to develop listening skills and be able to build up an atmosphere of openness, trust and goodwill in all their dealings with a school. A respect for confidentiality is essential to success as a consultant.

Evaluation

There is at present a lack of substantial evidence concerning the 'effectiveness' of training programmes for the heads and senior staff of secondary schools and there remains a considerable need for research in this field.

Difficulties

The task of evaluating training programmes is very complex because it is very difficult to identify and isolate those changes in individuals or schools which have been brought about by the training and those changes which may, in whole or in part, be attributed to other sources or influences. Changes in organization, in climate, in professional development and in job satisfaction are very difficult to measure.

Evaluation processes

Evaluation by questionnaire during or immediately after training is common and is valuable to course planners but limited by such factors as 'post-course euphoria'. It is impossible to study the long-term effects of training by such questionnaires. Some follow-up procedures in the form of further questionnaires or interviews are necessary to gain a longer-term perspective.

The results of evaluation programmes

The most effective evaluation programmes have been carried out in Sweden and in Northern Ireland.

(a) In Sweden, evaluation programmes have reported general changes in some schools, e.g., they have become more open and more democratic. There have been some similar changes in individuals and in the roles they play. However, large-scale changes have not been reported in schools, nor is there great optimism among the researchers. A long-term evaluation programme (1980–85) is now taking place in Sweden which should throw valuable light on the question of change in schools.

(b) In Northern Ireland, the findings suggest that a short course is only the initial stage in the training of heads as it can only create an awareness of the problems. Some form of follow-up is essential to change individuals or schools.

(c) These two evaluation programmes, although of very different training schemes, come to an important common conclusion that the major difficulty lies in relating a 'course' or a training programme to the 'reality' of a school. Heads experience considerable difficulty in returning to assume the role of a change agent while they are preoccupied with the task of maintaining day-to-day stability in schools.

(d) This confirms the writer's conclusion that the major problem that faces the heads of secondary schools is what may be described as the 'present-future dilemma'.

General conclusions

Such evidence as is available from existing evaluation programmes suggests that if changes are to be brought about in schools heads have an important part to play as change agents. To play this part they need training. Training programmes should aim to develop the *leadership skills* of the heads themselves but also aim to affect the school *directly*. The programme should help the head and the staff of the school to identify the changes which are necessary and also provide, if necessary, *support or consultant help* in implementing those changes over a period of time. Short courses will be inadequate for this purpose.

Such programmes need considerable resources and a national will to invest in the future. Given these conditions they may well prove to be the most effective method of changing heads and changing schools to match the changes which are taking place in society.

Bibliography

ASSOCIATION FOR TEACHER EDUCATION IN EUROPE AND NATIONAL ASSOCIATION OF HEADTEACHERS (1982). Training for Heads (School Leaders) in Europe. Report of conference, Gatwick, UK. Brussels: ATEE; Haywards Heath, W. Sussex: NAHT.

BARON, G. (1956). 'Some aspects of the "Headmaster Tradition"', *Researches and Studies,* **14,** 7–16. (Reprinted in: MUSGRAVE, P. W. (Ed) *Sociology, History and Education.* London: Methuen).

BATES, A.W. (1970. 'The administration of comprehensive schools'. In: MONKS, T.G. (Ed) *Comprehensive Education in Action.* Slough: NFER.

BENN, C. and SIMON, B. (1970). *Half Way There: A Report on the British Comprehensive School Reform.* London: McGraw Hill.

BENYON, L.M. (1982). The Training of Leaders of Educational Institutions in the Netherlands. North West Educational Management Centre, Fearnhead, Warrington (mimeographed).

BERNBAUM, G. (1973). 'Headmasters and schools: some preliminary findings', *Sociological Review,* **21,** 3, pp. 463–84.

BERNBAUM, G. (1976). 'The role of the head'. In: PETERS, R.S. (Ed) *The Role of the Head.* London: Routledge and Kegan Paul.

BOLAM, R. (1981). Strategies For Sustaining Educational Improvement in the 1980s. Paris: OECD/CERI (mimeographed).

BOLAM, R. (1982). Guidelines for Staff and External Consultants Working in GRIDS Project Schools. University of Bristol, School of Education.

BOLAM, R., SMITH, G. and CANTER, H. (1978). *LEA Advisers and the Mechanics of Innovation.* Windsor: NFER.

BRODGAARD, K. (1982). 'Denmark: courses for school leaders–a profile'. In: ASSOCIATION FOR TEACHER EDUCATION IN EUROPE and NATIONAL ASSOCIATION OF HEAD TEACHERS. Training for Heads (School Leaders) in Europe. Brussels: ATEE; Haywards Heath, W. Sussex: NAHT.

BUCKLEY, J.P. (1981). School Management Training in Sweden. Warrington: North West Educational Management Centre.

BUCKLEY, J.P. (1982). 'Current trends in school management'. In: COUNCIL OF EUROPE. *Current Trends in School Management.* Proceedings of the teachers' seminar held at Kristiansand, Norway, Oslo: Norwegian Ministry of Cultural and Scientific Affairs.

BURGOYNE, J., BOYDELL, T. and PEDLER, M. (1978). *Self-Development Theory and Applications for Practitioners.* London: Association of Teachers of Management.

BURNHAM, P.S. (1964). The role of the deputy head in secondary schools. Unpublished M.Ed. thesis, University of Leicester.

BURNHAM, P.S. (1968). 'The deputy-head'. In: ALLEN, B. (Ed) *Headship in the 1970s.* Oxford: Blackwell.

BUSH, T. *et al.* (Eds) (1980). *Approaches to School Management.* London: Harper and Row.

BUSH, T. and GETHINS, M. (1981). *Shorefields Comprehensive School.* Block 7 of Open University Course E323. Milton Keynes: Open University Press.

BYRNE, D., HINES, S. and McLEARY, L. (1978). *The Senior High School Principalship.* National survey, Vol. 1. Reston, Va.: National Association of Secondary School Principals.

COUNCIL OF EUROPE. COUNCIL FOR CULTURAL COOPERATION (1981). *How Pupils in Ten Schools in Europe are Prepared for Life.* Project No. 1: Preparation for life. Strasbourg: Council of Europe. DECS/EGT 19–E.

COUNCIL OF EUROPE. (1982). *Current Trends in School Management.* Proceedings of the teachers' seminar held at Kristiansand, Norway. Oslo: Norwegian Mininstry of Cultural and Scientific Affairs.

COUNCIL OF EUROPE. COUNCIL FOR CULTURAL COOPERATION (1983). *School Management Training in Europe.* Proceedings of the 12th Council of Europe teachers' seminar at Donaueschingen, Federal Republic of Germany. DECS/EGT (81)3. Strasbourg: Council of Europe.

DAVIES, T.P. (1983). Review and Institutional Development. Bromfield School, Wrexham, Clwyd (mimeographed).

EASTABROOK, G., and FULLAN, M. (1978). *School and Community: Principals and Community Schools in Ontario.* Toronto: Ontario Ministry of Education.

EKHOLM, M. (1976). Social Development in School: A Summary and Excerpts. Report No. 48 from the University of Göteborg, Institute of Education.

EKHOLM, M. (1977). School Leader Education in Sweden. Report No. 1 from School Leader Education, University of Linköping.

EKHOLM, M. (1979). Research in Education—does it matter? Report No. 3 from School Leader Education, University of Linköping.

EKHOLM, M. (1980). Evaluation of In-service Education of Teachers in Sweden—Results and Aspects of Future Evaluative Activities. Linköping: University of Linköping.

EKHOLM, M. (1981). 'How does the headmaster put what he has learnt into practice? Experiences with the Swedish training programme for headteachers'. In: COUNCIL OF EUROPE *School Management Training in Europe.* Proceedings of European Teachers' Seminar, Donaueschingen. DECS/EGT (81)3-E. Strasbourg: Council of Europe.

EKHOLM, M. (1983). 'Research on the school leader education programme in Sweden'. In: HEGARTY, S. (Ed) *Training for Management in Schools.* Windsor: NFER-NELSON for the Council of Europe.

ELLETT, C. (1976). *Results Oriented Management in Education. Final Report, Vol. 1.* Athens, Georgia: University of Georgia.

ESP, D.G. (1980). Selection and Training of Secondary School Headteachers in the Netherlands. Somerset Education Committee (mimeographed).

ESP, D.G. (1981). Training for Secondary School Headship in France. Somerset Education Committee (mimeographed).

ESP, D.G. (1982). 'Training approaches in various European countries—an overview'. In: HEGARTY, S. (Ed) *Training for Management in Schools.*

FLYNN, C.W. (1982). 'Towards collaborative decision-making in schools'. In: COUNCIL OF EUROPE. *Current Trends in School Management.* Proceedings of the teachers' seminar held at Kristiansand, Norway. Oslo: Norwegian Ministry of Cultural and Scientific Affairs.

FOY, N. (1979). 'Management education: current action and future needs', *Journal of European Industrial Training,* **3**, 2.

FRANCE. MINISTRY OF EDUCATION (1973). *Circulaire No. 73—525 du 10 Décembre 1973 aux Recteurs, aux Inspecteurs d'Académie. Objet: Stages de Formation des Futurs Chefs d'Etablissement Inscrits sur les Listes d'Aptitude. Paris: Ministry of Education.*

FRANCE. MINISTRY OF EDUCATION (1981). *Circulaire No. 81—006 du 23 Février 1981, aux Recteurs d'Académie. Objet: Formation Initiale et Continue des Chefs d'Etablissement et Personels de Direction des Lycées et Collèges. Paris: Ministry of Education.*

FULLAN, M. (1982). *The Meaning of Educational Change.* Toronto: OISE.

GIELEN, K.J.H. (1982). *Provision of Training for Heads (School Leaders) in the Netherlands.* Arnhem: School Organization and Management Group, Stichting Gelderse Leergangen.

GLATTER, R. (1972). *Management Development for the Education Profession.* London: Harrap.

GLATTER, R. (1980). 'School management in the 1980s', *Education,* **156**, 9, p. 216.

GLATTER, R. (1981). *Developing Staff for School Management.* Block 6, Part 6 of Open University course E323. Milton Keynes: Open University Press.

GLATTER, R. (1982). 'The micropolitics of education: issues for training', *Educational Management and Administration,* **10**, 2, pp. 160—5.

GLATTER, R. (1983). 'Implications of research policy on school management training'. In: HEGARTY, S. (Ed) *Training for Management in Schools.* Windsor: NFER-NELSON for the Council of Europe.

GONZALEZ-TIRADOS, R.M. (1982). 'A programme for the training of school directors at the Polytechnic University of Madrid'. In: HEGARTY, S. (Ed) *Training for Management in Schools.* Windsor: NFER-NELSON for the Council of Europe.

GORTON, R., and McINTYRE, K. (1978). *The Senior High School Principalship: The Effective Principal. Vol. 2.* Reston, Va.: The National Association of Secondary School Principals.

GREAT BRITAIN. DEPARTMENT OF EDUCATION AND SCIENCE (1977). *Ten Good Schools: A Secondary School Enquiry.* London: HMSO.

GROSS, N., GIAQUINTA, J.B., and BERNSTEIN, M. (1971). *Implementing Organisational Innovation.* New York: Harper and Row.

HANDY, C.B. (1976). *Understanding Organisations.* London: Penguin.

HAVELOCK, R. (1973). *The Change Agent's Guide to Innovation in Education.* New York, Englewood Cliffs: Educational Technology Publications.

HEGARTY, S. (1983). 'A view from the rapporteur'. In: HEGARTY, S. (Ed) *Training for Management in Schools.* Windsor: NFER-NELSON for the Council of Europe.

HEGARTY, S. (Ed) (1983). *Training for Management in Schools.* Windsor: NFER–NELSON for the Council of Europe.

HELT, J.P. (1982). 'The training of headteachers in France'. In: ASSOCIATION FOR TEACHER EDUCATION IN EUROPE and NATIONAL ASSOCIATION OF HEADTEACHERS Training for Heads (School Leaders) in Europe. Brussels: ATEE; Haywards Heath, W. Sussex: NAHT.

HILL, P., WACHITECH, J. and WILLIAMS, R. (1980). *The Effects of Federal Education Programmes on School Principles.* Santa Monica, California: Rand Corporation.

HOPES, C. (Ed) (1981). European Forum on Educational Administration: *Report on the Intervisitation Programme in the Federal Republic of Germany.* Frankfurt: Deutsches Institut für Internationale Pädagogische Forschung. (Available in English).

HOPES, C. (1982). 'Professional development of school management in the Federal Republic of Germany'. In: ASSOCIATION FOR TEACHER EDUCATION IN EUROPE and

NATIONAL ASSOCIATION OF HEADTEACHERS Training for Heads (School Leaders) in Europe. Brussels: ATEE; Haywards Heath, W. Sussex: NAHT.

HOPES, C. (1983). 'Problems of relating selection criteria and training needs—research and evaluation attempts in the Federal Republic of Germany'. In: HEGARTY, S. (Ed) *Training for Management in Schools*. Windsor: NFER-NELSON for the Council of Europe.

HOUSE, E., and LAPAN, S. (1978). *Survival in the Classroom*. Boston: Allyn and Bacon.

HUGHES, M.G. (1972). The role of the secondary school head. Unpublished Ph.D thesis, University of Wales.

HUGHES, M.G. (1973). 'The professional-as-administrator: the case of the secondary school head', *Education Administration Bulletin*, **2**, (i).

HUGHES, M.G. (1975). 'The innovating school head: autocratic initiator or catalyst of cooperation', *Education Administration*, **4**, (i).

HUGHES, M.G. (1977). 'Consensus and conflict about the role of the secondary head', *British Journal of Educational Studies*, **25**, (i).

HUGHES, M.G. (1978). 'Reconciling professional and administrative concerns'. In: BUSH, T. *et al.* (Eds) *Approaches to School Management*. London: Harper and Row.

HUGHES, M.G. (1983). 'The role and tasks of heads of schools in England and Wales: research studies and professional development provision'. In: HEGARTY, S. (Ed) *Training for Management in Schools*. Windsor: NFER-NELSON for the Council of Europe.

HUGHES, M.G., CARTER, J., and FIDLER, B. (1981). Professional Development Provision for Senior Staff in Schools and Colleges. Birmingham: University of Birmingham, Department of Social and Administrative Studies, Faculty of Education.

HULTMAN, G. (1981). Organisation Development Through Management Training: An Evaluation of the First Cadres of the Swedish School Leader Training. Linköping: University of Linköping, (Swedish: English summary.)

JACKSON, A. (1976). Heading For What? University of Leeds

Counselling and Development Unit, Department of Psychology, University of Leeds (mimeographed).

KATZ, D., and KHAN, R. (1978). *The Social Psychology of Organisations.* 2nd Edn. New York: Wiley.

KATZ, R.L. (1974). 'Skills of an effective administrator', *Harvard Business Review,* **52**, Sept.–Oct., pp. 90–102.

KING, R. (1968). 'The headteacher and his authority'. In: ALLEN, B. (Ed) *Headship in the 1970s.* Oxford: Blackwell.

KOLB, D.A., RUBIN, I.M., and McINTYRE, J.M. (1971). *Organizational Psychology: An Experiential Approach.* Hemel Hempstead: Prentice Hall International.

KVIST, P. (1982a). Working Conditions and Leadership in Schools, (AMS): An Innovation Project. Report available from: Skoledirectøren; Bjøgvin, Strandgt. 221, Bergen, Norway.

KVIST, P. (1982b). 'Norway–the innovation project AMS'. In: ASSOCIATION FOR TEACHER EDUCATION IN EUROPE and NATIONAL ASSOCIATION OF HEAD TEACHERS Training for Heads (School Leaders) in Europe. Brussels: ATEE; Haywards Heath, W. Sussex: NAHT.

KVIST, P. (1982c). 'Leadership in schools: a Norwegian programme for improvement'. In: WATSON, L.E. (Ed) *Sheffield Papers in Educational Management.* Sheffield: Sheffield City Polytechnic.

LEGRAND, L. FRANCE. MINISTRY OF EDUCATION (1983). *Pour un Collège Démocratique.* Paris: La Documentation Française.

LYONS, G. (1972). 'Patterns of administrative work in secondary schools', *Educational Administration Bulletin,* **1**, 1.

LYONS, G. (1976). *Heads' Tasks: A Handbook of Secondary School Administration.* Slough: NFER.

MARCH, J.G. (1974). 'Analytical skills and the university training of administrators', *Journal of Educational Administration,* **12**, 1 (May).

MARTIN, W.J. and WILLOWER, D.J. (1981). 'The managerial behaviour of high school principals', *Educational Administration Quarterly,* **17**, 1, pp. 69–90.

191

MINTZBERG, H. (1973). *The Nature of Managerial Work.* New York: Harper and Row.

MINTZBERG, H. (1975). 'The manager's job: folklore and fact', *Harvard Business Review,* **53**, 4, pp. 49–61.

MORGAN, C. (1981). NASSP Assessment Centre. An Internal Working Paper of the POST Project on the Selection of Secondary Head Teachers. Open University, Milton Keynes.

MORGAN, C., and HALL, V. (1982). 'The POST Project. What is the job of the secondary school head?' *Education,* 159, 25, i–iv (18th June).

NETHERLANDS, THE. MINISTRY OF EDUCATION AND SCIENCE. *Secondary School Teacher Training in The Netherlands. Docinform 300 E.* The Hague: Ministry of Education and Science.

NJERVE, I. (1982). 'Evaluation of a school-based development project in the County of Hordaland, Norway: an interim report'. In: HEGARTY, S. (Ed) *Training for Management in Schools.* Windsor: NFER-NELSON for the Council of Europe.

NJERVE, I., OSNES, J., and VAVIK, L. (1983). Working Milieu and School Development: An Evaluation Project in the County of Hordaland, Norway. Report available from Stord College of Education, 5414 Rommetveit, Norway.

NOCKELS, A. (1981). The Problems, Issues and Strategies of the First Year of a Secondary Headship. A report to the Oxfordshire Education Committee (mimeographed).

NORTH WEST EDUCATIONAL MANAGEMENT CENTRE (1978). 1972–1977: A Review of the First Five Years of the Centre. Report obtainable from the Centre at North Cheshire College, Fearnhead, Warrington.

O'SHEA, A.T. (1983). *Management in Secondary Education: An Evaluation of the Department of Education's Programme of Training in Educational Management for Principals of Post-primary Schools in Northern Ireland.* Belfast: Northern Ireland Council for Education Research.

PAUTLER, E. (1982). INSET for School Leaders. Proceedings of the seminar for school administrators: 'School for the 11–14 Age

Range and its Priority Tasks' at Pont-à-Mousson, France. Commission of the European Communities, Brussels, V/2097/82–EN.

PERETTI, A. de, (1982). *Rapport au Ministre de l'Education Nationale de la Commission sur la Formation des Personnels de l'Education Nationale.* Paris: La Documentation Française.

ROYSELAND, A. (1982). 'A school without a headteacher: collective leadership'. In: COUNCIL OF EUROPE. *Current Trends in School Management.* Oslo: Norwegian Ministry of Cultural and Scientific Affairs.

RUTTER, M., MAUGHAN, B., MORTIMORE, P. and OUSTON, J. (1979). *Fifteen Thousand Hours.* London: Open Books.

SARASON, S. (1971). *The Culture of the School and the Problem of Change.* Boston: Allyn and Bacon.

SCHMITZ, K. (1980). 'Gegenwärtige Probleme–dargestellt am Wochenlauf eines Schulleiters', *Bildung und Erziehung,* **33,** 6.

SCHMUCK, R.A. (1981). A Summary of School-Based Change Strategies: The State of the Art. IMTEC, Oslo, Norway.

SCHMUCK, R.A. and RUNKEL, P. (1977). (Eds). *The Second Handbook of Organizational Development in Schools.* Palo Alto: Mayfield Pub. Co.

SCHOFIELD, J. (1980). The Creation of a Good Comprehensive School. A report to the City of Manchester Education Committee.

SELJELID, T. (1982). Handbook for *The Working Environment and the Running of the School (AMS).* Oslo: Ministry of Cultural and Scientific Affairs.

SKOGLUND, O. (1982). 'Reflections on the headteacher's role and responsibility in a democratic school community'. In: COUNCIL OF EUROPE. *Current Trends in School Management.* Oslo: Norwegian Ministry of Cultural and Scientific Affairs.

STEGÖ, N.E. (1978). The Role of the School Leader. Report No. 2 from School Leader Education, Linköping University.

STEGÖ, N.E. (1979). Training School Leaders in Sweden. Report No. 4 from School Leader Education, Linköping University.

STEGÖ, N.E. (1982). 'Training school leaders in Sweden'. In: ASSOCIATION FOR TEACHER EDUCATION IN EUROPE and NATIONAL ASSOCIATION OF HEADTEACHERS Training for Heads (School Leaders) in Europe. Brussels: ATEE; Haywards Heath, W. Sussex: NAHT.

SWEDISH NATIONAL BOARD OF EDUCATION (1975). SIA: The Working Environment of the School. A summary of the report by Rolf Beckne, Information Section, S 10642 Stockholm.

THOM, D. (1979). 'Administration without ulcers: a leadership concept for these times', *Comment on Education*. A publication from the Guidance Centre, Governing Council of the University of Toronto.

TODD, R. and DENNISON, W.F. (1978). 'The changing role of the deputy headteacher in English secondary schools', *Educational Review*, **30**, 3.

TOUSSAINT, C. FRANCE. MINISTRY OF EDUCATION (1978). *Rapport sur les Equipes Académiques d'animation et de la Vie Scolaire*. Paris: La Documentation Française.

TURNER, L.T. (1981). Preparation for headship. B. Phil (Ed) dissertation, University of Birmingham.

VANBERGEN, P. (1977). The School and its Relations with the Community. Council of Europe contribution to the Tenth European Conference of Ministers of Education, CME/X, 77, 3. Strasbourg.

VAN HEES, T. (1982). 'The provision of training for heads (school leaders) in the Netherlands'. In: ASSOCIATION FOR TEACHER EDUCATION IN EUROPE and NATIONAL ASSOCIATION OF HEADTEACHERS Training for Heads (School Leaders) in Europe. Brussels: ATEE; Haywards Heath, W. Sussex: NAHT.

WELDY, G. (1979). *Principals: what they do and who they are*. Reston, Va.: National Association of Secondary School Principals.

WILLIS, Q. (1980). 'The work activities of school principals: an observational study', *Journal of Educational Administration*, **18**, 1.

WILLIAMS, H. (1979). The role of the deputy head: is it changing? B. Phil dissertation, University of Birmingham.